Everyday Conversations with Matthew

Everyday Conversations with Matthew

John Holdsworth

scm press

© John Holdsworth 2019

Published in 2019 by SCM Press
Editorial office 3rd Floor, Invicta House,
108–114 Golden Lane,
London EC1Y 0TG, UK
www.scmpress.co.uk

SCM Press is an imprint of Hymns Ancient & Modern Ltd
(a registered charity)

Hymns Ancient & Modern® is a registered trademark of
Hymns Ancient & Modern Ltd
13A Hellesdon Park Road, Norwich, Norfolk NR6 5DR, UK

British Library Cataloguing in Publication data

A catalogue record for this book is available
from the British Library

978 0 334 05746 8

Typeset by Manila Typesetting Company
Printed and bound by CPI Group (UK) Ltd

Contents

Acknowledgements

This book maintains my passion for a means of communicating Bible content that speaks to real situations in our world. It reflects conversations that have actually happened, and I am grateful for the opportunities to hold them. I am grateful also to church study groups in Limassol (Cyprus), Al Ain and Jebel Ali (UAE), who have 'test run' the material and helped with its revision. Bishop Michael Lewis and Professor Leslie Francis have both been gracious enough to read the text at various stages and offer their comments as critical friends. Among others who have played an enabling part I would like to thank Anetta Stylianou and Helen Perry for their support, professionally; and Veronika Svitkova for her support domestically.

Introduction:
Starting a Conversation

Nowadays, it seems, Matthew has fewer friends than he once had. If you like, fewer people want to talk to him or to engage with him in the kind of conversation that might lead to development of faith, Christian understanding or formation. In the early days, his was the most popular Gospel, but that is no longer the case.

Mark has a very direct and appealing style and is quite a lot shorter than the other three, and that makes him attractive to some. Luke gives us a flowing narrative that is both easy to read and memorable. Also, Matthew lacks the spiritual poetic quality with which John appeals to others.

I have tried to imagine the kind of people who might benefit from trying to talk with Matthew today, and each chapter of this book begins by describing one or more of them. The kind of people who will benefit most might identify with someone from among their number. Their questions are based on a desire to match experience with faith.

They are not particularly interested in ancient history or the Middle Eastern culture of thousands of years ago, but they do want to know more about themselves, about God and about how faith communities function at their best. Especially they want to know more about Jesus. They probably suspect that finding out more about him, his teaching and significance, may well help to mould or change their world view, their attitudes and choices, and perhaps contribute to their development as fully formed human beings.

Matthew does catch our attention in some ways. The Beatitudes and the Lord's Prayer are best known in their Matthean form. The parable of the wheat and the tares and the story of the three wise men are also well known. But there is also a sense that as a relationship partner, Matthew is somewhat 'needy'. This is not just a question of style. It has to do also with theological approach. Commentators on his Gospel sometimes feel the need to apologize in advance for the assumed inaccessibility of the theological thought forms for the modern reader (Fenton 1963, pp. 17–26, for example).

This book takes some things for granted in its readers. It begins where modern scholarship has brought us, with an understanding that, although having a common purpose, each of the Synoptic Gospels is an individual and crafted attempt to make the Christian message about Jesus relevant to its own community in its own time, raising the question: if that is so, is Matthew's Gospel at all relevant to a society such as ours? It also takes for granted appreciations of the literary skills of each of the Gospel writers as they pursue their rhetorical and apologetic task of persuading readers that what they have to say really matters. So we are entitled to ask of the Gospel, as we engage with it, the kind of questions we might ask in a book club about any literary work, concerning how the writer achieves his purpose.

Each chapter opens a conversation which then continues throughout it. The exercises enable a further conversation to emerge if the book is being read as part of a group project, though it can equally well take place with an individual reader. To make things easier and more accessible, the book follows the order of events in the Gospel, and so can be used as an aid to a sequential reading. We want to try to find Jesus as Matthew wants us to see him and, crucially along the way, judge whether there are particular insights that might resource our underlying aim of allowing Jesus to be an influence in our lives. This is a conversation related to everyday concerns and the hope is that it will continue after the book is finished.

Studying the New Testament does not simply mean studying what other people have said about it. It means seeing for yourself and, in the process, gaining confidence in handling the text. The exercises are designed to get beneath the skin of the text and arguments about it, to see how it might relate to our own situation and experience. The Reading List at the end of the book aims to connect the reader with the wider community of scholarship, and this too should not be ignored. Particular emphasis will be given to classic texts and to the writings that are accessible. At the end of the book I hope it will be clear that reading Matthew is a matter of entering into a conversation with someone to whom Jesus meant much; and trying to find out why it mattered to him and why it matters to us.

I

Painting Jesus by Numbers

Chris is a relatively recent Christian. Now in her twenties, she was not brought up in a family that would have described itself as religious. Her first real contact with Christians was being invited to a service held in a converted supermarket that attracted large numbers of people within her own age group and proved to be an eye-opener in other ways as well. There was a stage with musicians and a presenter. The music was contemporary and there was a great atmosphere. Chris quickly made friends there and felt at one with the general ethos of the message she heard delivered each week. However, as a graduate in economics, she felt she ought to be learning about core faith documents at first hand for herself before signing up completely. She decided to start with the Gospels and, since it was first, with Matthew, but was soon dismayed by the first couple of chapters. The author seemed to be making every effort to put her off. As a graduate, she has respect for scholarship and her question is a cry for help to scholars: she wants to start a conversation that asks: how can you help me read Matthew in a way that connects with my experience of Church, and with the deeper questions about life that they talk about there?

Chris is not alone in her dismay. Academic commentators on Matthew's Gospel are well aware of how distant it can feel from our own times and assumptions. John Fenton goes so far as to make a list of the problems the Gospel presents for the modern reader (Fenton 1963, pp. 17–26), and some commentaries read as if the author is quite overwhelmed by them. Difficulties include matters of style and presentation and methods of argument that we do not nowadays find compelling. Additionally, there are issues that arise from the message itself with its emphasis on end times and judgement, its treatment of rewards and punishment, and its uncompromising vitriol against Jewish religious leaders.

In the Introduction to her commentary, Anna Case-Winters asks: 'Why Matthew? Why now?' (Case-Winters 2015, p. 1) and approaches the Gospel from a direction unimpeded by questions around style. She locates the book in what she decides is its historic context within the infant Christian community. 'In these texts', she says, 'we see Jesus facing up to conflict and controversy, ministering at the margins, overturning presuppositions about insiders and outsiders, privileging the powerless, demonstrating the authority of ethical leadership, challenging allegiance to empire and pointing the way to a wider, divine embrace than many dared imagine' (p. 1).

Case-Winters' approach displays a frustration with the kind of commentary that deals at length with the question, for example, of whether the Christian community for which Matthew was writing was made up mostly of former Jews or mostly of Gentiles, without telling us why that should matter to us. In this context 'us' is the modern Church community – people like Chris. She translates that critical question into a description of a time 'when there was conflict and division in the community of faith', and 'when some were insiders and some were outsiders' (p. 1). In other words, she combines *exegesis* – the traditional method of interpreting texts based on reading out from what the text says and trying to get behind its original meaning – with *eisegesis. Eisegesis* starts with contemporary experience and looks at the text to see whether that experience can be mirrored there. In other words, it reads *in* instead of, or as well as, reading *out*. This is an approach which is much more likely to feed Chris's appetite. Case-Winters' list is not exhaustive though and it is tempting to add to the list of contemporary issues that we might recognize in the Gospel.

Perhaps one very important one concerns institutions. Matthew certainly has much to say about the institutions of Jewish religion. He is hugely critical of religious leaders and what passes for religious liturgy and observance. Based as it is on religious principles, this has implications for his understanding of law, and its demands, and perhaps even on the whole question of Jewish identity. He clearly has an agenda here and sees in Jesus the remedy he seeks. So what is the basic problem?

It could be argued that it is a very modern problem, sometimes described in terms of 'reputational damage' – that is, when the reputation of an institution is deemed more important than the pursuit of its supposed core values. For example, when abuse allegations in a church are covered up because the institution's reputation is considered more important than the damage to the abused. Or when, in wider society, wrongdoing in a public body, such as the police or politicians or aid agencies, is covered up to protect the reputation of those institutions. These are all institutions whose core values commit them to the care and protection of the vulnerable, but sometimes they are justly accused of having developed to a point where that vision has been overtaken by an institutional dynamic that demands protection. This is all the more dangerous when those institutions carry with them power, and particularly the power to shape identity.

Those who are concerned about this widespread modern phenomenon are extremely critical of leadership that lacks moral courage. They are among those who urge a 'back to basics' approach to remind those institutions of what they truly represent and the values they are meant to hold. These are values that are crucial for society, and no institution, it is claimed, should be deemed too big to fail because of its power, its place in society or its place in national consciousness and identity. It could be argued that this is Matthew's mission too.

To do

Is this a picture of society that you recognize? Do you feel comfortable in beginning study of a Bible passage from these kinds of considerations?

Such considerations may whet our appetite for Matthew and encourage us to be more tolerant of its style as we try to find ways of reading that enable us to get under its skin, but we still have to come to terms with its peculiar presentation. How might we get a handle on that?

In a determined, but ultimately doomed, attempt to encourage me to be an artist, well-meaning rel- atives used to make me childhood presents of the craft activity called 'painting by numbers'. The idea was (and is) that a colourful picture would be reduced to a delineated plan of the distribution of each of the colours. The craft element was then to apply numbered paints to the equivalent numbered sections on the picture outline in order to recreate a beautiful coloured picture. Inevitably the result differed from a work of original art (in my case very greatly). Original art often does not have distinct lines but its hues and colours shade in subtle sophistication. By contrast, a painting by numbers picture, even at best, has a more formal and strict appearance. It seems to relate less to the world of art than to some more mathematical or scientific discipline.

To do

Think for a moment about the truths you most rely on for meaning in your life. Then think about how you know that they are true. Are you reassured by scientific and evidence-based means of truth, in which case, what is the evidence that supports what you rely on? Is truth for you something less tangible, in which case how would you describe it? Do the most important truths rely more on faith than certainty? You may need quite some time to think about these questions, but they are central to the way we respond to the different Gospel presentations, each of which seek to persuade us of what the authors in each case believe to be fundamental truth.

Of the four Gospels, it might well be helpful to see Luke or John as works of original art in that sense; and if so, by comparison, to see Matthew as more strict, formal and, perhaps, even more academic.

It could be said to attempt to paint a picture of Jesus by numbers, fitting the stories about him into pre-designed shapes. So where did the pre-designing come from? One convincing answer would be, from Jewish tradition. Throughout the Gospel there is ample evidence that the writer is familiar with Old Testament writing and, in particular, that he inter- prets that writing in terms of the expectation of a Messiah. He also understands contemporary Jewish culture. But beyond the evidence of what Matthew writes is the evidence of how he arranges what he writes. For the past hundred years or so it has been generally accepted that there is an intentional structure to the Gospel that mirrors Jewish literary convention.

The repeated phrase 'after these sayings' occurs five times at the conclusion of collections of mate- rial, much of which is not collected in the same way in other Gospels. In other words, the suggestion is that Matthew has brought together in a *thematic* way material that is presented in a different way in the other Gospels where it occurs, and has done so five times. B. W. Bacon (Bacon 1930) suggested that this arrangement determines the structure of the Gospel as a whole, and that each of the discourses is preceded by a narrative section, so producing five 'books' that would be equivalent to a kind of Christian Pentateuch. The arrangement of books in fives is well attested in the Old Testament as well as in other Jewish literature. It can be seen in both the Psalms and Proverbs, for example, as well as in the Torah, otherwise known as the Pentateuch, the first section of the Hebrew Bible and the first five books of the Christian Old Testament. The detail of this view has been challenged, but the five-fold pattern of discourses is an inescapable fact. However, it is not the only possibility of structural engineering suggested by a repeated phrase.

J. D. Kingsbury (1975) noted the repetition of the phrase 'from that time Jesus began . . .' at 4.17 and 16.21 and suggested that on each occasion they introduced a new intentional section of the Gospel. This would produce a three-part structure. At this point we do not need to look at the proposed contents of these sections, but rather to note that there does appear to be an intended formal structure to Matthew, and that it may conform to Jewish conventions surrounding the numbers three and five.

The many quotations from the Old Testament bear witness not only to the author's knowledge of the tradition but also to a way of presenting Jesus that puts a great premium on evidence-based truth. This also accords with the more scientific approach that we have already noted. Matthew aims to convince his audience by relating episodes in the life of Jesus to Old Testament prophecies as he understands and interprets them. One almost expects to see QED at the end of some sections. If our aim is to find a human Jesus with whom we can identify, clearly we shall have to read between the lines.

To do

There is a series of humorous books that attempts to describe complex human conditions in the manner of a car manual (see B. Starling, 2016, *Haynes Explains Marriage: Owners Workshop Manual*, Haynes, London. Others in the series describe pensioners or teenagers. You get the point). You may be able to get hold of a copy, but whether you can or not, what do you think are the limitations of this approach with regard to religious practice? Does a Manual to explain Religion have advantages?

At this point it may be useful to let Matthew speak for himself. The first two chapters of the book are only found in Matthew. They are his particular introduction. They act as a kind of formal overture to the symphony that will be the Gospel, rehearsing its themes, teasing the reader with what will follow, introducing the presentation of Jesus, which will be its central intention. We might be tempted to begin at 1.18, and to dismiss the genealogy which begins the work, simply because it's boring to read, but that would be to miss some important clues, and to fail to recognize the textbook-like presentation. Nowadays textbooks in many disciplines include tables, graphs and boxed sections of interpretation. That was not available to Matthew, and this is his equivalent.

Read Matthew 1.1–17

The first clue is not evident in English translation, and that is that the Greek word used for genealogy is *genesis* and in fact the whole line is a direct quotation of the Greek version of Genesis 2.4. Just as the Gospel of John begins with an overt reference to the Genesis account of creation, so Matthew immediately suggests a link to the beginnings of the story, but which story? The answer is given immediately afterwards. This is the story of Israel beginning with Abraham. It will be immediately apparent that the genealogy is contrived in a number of ways. The most obvious is that there are not enough people there for this to be an actual family tree. Luke also includes a genealogy in his Gospel, which is completely different and much longer. It has been suggested that Matthew's genealogy is based on significant figures and events in the story of Israel, and that it is closely related to the idea of kingship, witness the pointed mention of David. Just as some monarchs have a 'real' birthday and an official birthday, so perhaps Jesus as king has a real genealogy and an 'official' one.

For an 'official' genealogy this one has some surprising entrants. In the first section, we have four women who are all controversial in some way. Tamar acted as a prostitute in order to secure children and shame her father in law (Genesis 38). Rahab, the harlot of Jericho (Joshua 2.1–21), saved the lives of two spies – the original tart with a heart – but hardly a role model to be claimed in a royal genealogy. Both were Canaanites. Bathsheba is mentioned in passing. She was married to a Hittite and so she may well have been one, but she is best remembered for David's shameful act in which they both committed adultery, and its considerable aftermath (2 Samuel 11 and following). Perhaps more damaging than that is the mention of Ruth (1.5). Morally she was blameless but a whole book had been written about her by this time, not yet part of holy scripture but certainly well known, demonstrating that someone as close to David as his great grandmother was a foreigner, a Moabitess. The final woman to be mentioned is Mary, and at this point the whole scandal of the genealogy is revealed. What we have been reading is, if regarded as a truthful family tree, the genealogy of Joseph, who has nothing genetically to do with Jesus. Mary too is, as the next chapter will reveal, a suspicious character at this point in the story, as someone pregnant but unmarried.

The artificial nature of the genealogy is emphasized by the summary comment that 14 generations separate each of the three periods of Israelite history. To understand the significance of that, we have to remember that within contemporary Jewish literary practice, one genre which influenced Matthew's writing was that of apocalyptic. We shall have opportunity, as we progress, to see various instances of how this fairly complex genre is more evident in this Gospel than elsewhere. Apocalyptic is a way of writing about destiny. From a theological standpoint it is a way of saying that just as God has created the physical world, so also he has created the structure for human society, and has designed a history in which that society will fulfil God's purposes.

Apocalyptic writers looked for clues as to how that history was organized and how it might develop. They did this in a kind of scientific way that must have appealed to Matthew. They looked at the evidence for divisions within history and saw that God had created seven days. They deduced that seven was thus a very important number in understanding the creation/history plan. Within apocalyptic writing the number seven and its derivatives assumed great significance. Seven came to be regarded as the number of God himself and so the number of perfection and completeness. Three is also an important number since it can express intensity. So to describe that which is wholly God could be given the code 777. That which might appear to be God, but actually turns out to be an impostor, at its most intense would be 666.

For our purposes the number 14, as twice times seven, is describing God's creative work in designing and maintaining history. These numbers might not be accurate, but what they point to is a statement of faith about God and history, about the progress of the bit of history that people were in at that present (the 'present age'), and the significance of Jesus in all that. The David theme is also evident in the number, in that Hebrew letters operate rather like Roman numerals – each letter has a numerical value. The word David in Hebrew is made up of three letters, DVD. The value of D is four. The value of V is six. Hence the total value of DVD is 14, at which point you sense a QED coming.

To do

Compare the passage we have been considering with Luke 3.23–38. What differences are there between the two? Bearing in mind the discussion above, what differences do you think this might lead to in the interpretation of Jesus's significance?

The other point that English translations often miss is that in Greek the opening sentence begins: 'the book of the genealogy of Jesus Christ . . .' The first three Gospels each introduce their content in different ways. Mark describes his as 'the beginning of the good news/Gospel of Jesus Christ' (Mark 1.1). Luke's initial introduction does not mention Jesus by name but describes what follows as 'an orderly account' (Luke 1.3). Matthew is writing a book. That designation, along with the style and approach we have already noticed, has led commentators to think of Matthew as a textbook or a manual for some specific teaching purpose. Paul Minear (1984) speaks of a Teacher's Gospel. Krister Stendahl had in mind a School of St Matthew, whose role was to provide an interpretative commentary on the Old Testament texts. He was writing at the time when the Dead Sea Scrolls had been discovered, and he saw similarities between Matthew and some of the scrolls, particularly the commentary on Habakkuk. Others believe the presentation was to provide easily memorable passages for catechumens. Matthew was the most popular and oft-quoted Gospel in the early records available to us. Within the New Testament a number of similarities have been noted between the Gospel and the Letter of James, for example, a Letter which stresses the practical aspects of Christian faith.

The opening line identifies Jesus as the Christ. This conveys more than we might expect. The word Christ is a translation of the Hebrew Messiah, meaning anointed one, and so refers to a king like David. The anointing is a sign of God's favour and investiture. But in apocalyptic writing, a tradition had developed which had a special role for the Messiah. This writing sought to find order in history, and did so by dividing history into 'ages'. One of the themes of apocalyptic was describing how one age would give way to another. This was inevitably tied up with a message of hope that the new age would repair the deficiencies of the old. There would be new individuals with a new heart. There would be new communities committed to peace and justice, and even creation itself would be renewed to make it a safer and more perfect context for all living creatures (for a full treatment see Gowan 2000, pp. 21–120). This was an attractive message for people who were suffering, depressed or without hope. Some apocalyptic traditions believed that the new age would be ushered in by the new Messiah of God, the new Christ. So to describe Jesus as Christ in the first sentence of the Gospel is to declare that a new king like David has indeed been raised by God to usher in the new age.

Read Matthew 1.18–25

This account of the birth is noticeably shorter than Luke's. It begins by using the same word in Greek, *genesis*, to describe the birth. No explanatory narrative is offered, except Joseph's dream. However, there is an explanation of the reason for naming the boy Jesus – he will save his people. This would have needed no explanation for Jews, who were well used to names being descriptions of people's character or purpose, and indeed an example is given of that in the quote from Isaiah 7.14. Actually, Jesus is not called Emmanuel. He is never again referred to by that name, but in the very last verse of the Gospel there may be an overt reference to Jesus's vocation in terms of being 'God with Us', in that he promises to be with us to the end of the age (28.20).

This is the first example of Matthew's use of proof texts or *logia*. There is a proliferation of them in chapter 2. It is noticeable that the majority of these *logia* come at the beginning and end of the

Gospel. Each is introduced with a similar formula. Matthew's exegesis of the Isaiah passage bears no relation to its original context or to the fact that Hebrew has two words for describing young women: one for virgin in the technical sense and one that might correspond to the English word 'damsel'. Greek only has the one word to translate both of these. The original sense of 'damsel' is thus transferred to the more technical sense of virgin. That is not to cast doubt on the virgin tradition which is clearly widespread (as in Luke's account: this is one of the few things the accounts have in common), but simply to demonstrate Matthew's enthusiasm for proving his point no matter what the details might demand, and his (quasi-scientific) need to find a cause for every event.

To do

Have a look at a collection of Christmas carols. Of those which attempt to tell the Bible story, try to find one that is more faithful to Matthew's account. Which account do they generally rely on, Matthew or Luke? Why do you think that is?

Read Matthew 2

Knowing Matthew's sense of order, it should be the case that the first passage in which he describes the events immediately post-birth has particular significance. Some of that significance is overt in a further selection of proof texts, although there is no apparent Old Testament source for the last one (2.23). Some scholars think that quite a lot of this chapter is the product of Matthew's imagination, having reflected on the Old Testament promises, but indeed the whole sequence is quite imaginable. Other signifiers are less obvious. Isaiah 60.1–3 seems to be fulfilled in the coming of the astrologers (Matthew does not call them kings) at the king's behest. The flight to Egypt is interesting, with the text from Hosea (11.1). The text originally refers to Israel as God's son, and it was originally Israel that emerged from Egypt, according to the Exodus tradition, to settle the land of Israel. What seems to be suggested here is that Jesus not only assumes the historic kingship and not only assumes the vocation that that kingship involves in terms of saving his people, but that in some sense, in his own person, he embodies all that the historic Israel was to God and perhaps even supersedes that relationship. This would be a huge claim.

One consequence of declaring that Jesus was in effect the new Israel would be to completely undermine the securities, assumed privileges and presumed election of those who were able to claim an ethnic descent as Semitic Jews. This would in effect say to religious Jews: the important thing is not whether you are Jewish and attempt to keep the law and think salvation comes in that way. The important thing is that you are a member of Christ, and follow his new law. That is a definite theme in what follows.

Matthew goes out of his way to tease us with parallels to the Moses story. Herod slays all the children in the way that the Pharaoh got rid of male children after the birth of Moses (Exodus 1.15, 22). It could be said that just as Moses has an unusual birth and is then sheltered from slaughter, so Jesus, ironically by going to Egypt, is sheltered from slaughter. This is a comparison that will be developed. The reference to Rachel points us to Jeremiah 31.15 and to Ramah where the Exiles were gathered prior to their deportation to Babylon (Jeremiah 40.1). Once again we see the Exodus and Exile themes punctuating the story.

So what do these two chapters lead us to expect?

At this point perhaps we need to stand back from the text a little and think about Matthew as a person of faith trying to communicate with a particular audience and trying to persuade them that what he was to tell them would be both good and news. What do we know of the author and what do we know of his audience? Can we identify with either?

In fact we know little of Matthew. It is unlikely that he was a disciple, since his account relies so much on Mark and Q rather than on personal recollection, but it is not impossible. In any case all we know about that Matthew is that he was a tax collector, entertained Jesus on occasion and was a disciple. Most of what he reveals about himself, whoever he was, he reveals through his work.

To do

Which of the following descriptions of the author would you think justified from what we have read so far?

- Scholar.
- Jewish Christian.
- Christian Jew (slightly different emphasis – see below).
- Community leader.
- Nationalist zealot.
- Man of the people.

See how and if your view changes as we proceed through the book.

There is some external evidence that points to a geographical location for the writing of the Gospel somewhere between Galilee and Syrian Antioch. Most commentators opt for a location somewhere in the borderlands between the two. There is a general consensus that Matthew is writing for a particular community, and that this is not written as a Gospel for general use. That suggests that since the author clearly had access to the Gospel of Mark, he did not think that Gospel was sufficient for his community. Either it did not answer the questions they were asking, or its tone and cultural background were foreign, or Matthew wanted to present a different theological standpoint. Perhaps all three of those reasons are true.

The questions for us are rather: who would have understood what Matthew was describing; and, what situation does the text lead us to conjecture? The answer to the first is universally accepted as Jewish converts to the cause of Jesus. However in order to answer the second we have to be aware of the subtle differences between describing them as Jewish Christians or Christian Jews. In AD 85, a curse was inserted into the synagogue liturgy against 'Nazarenes and heretics' which led to the widespread exclusion of Christian-leaning Jews from synagogues. This was make your mind up time.

We might imagine the situation in the UK three hundred years ago when a movement called Methodism emerged within the Anglican Church. There came a point where for one reason or another the movement became a Church in its own right. At that point there was a division in congregations and people had to decide which identity they chose. That choice had political and social consequences. So it was for Christians expelled from the synagogues. The situations are not exactly parallel. Methodists were not cursed, but UK religious history is not without its own history of persecution, such as that experienced after AD 85 and, locally, before that time, by Jewish converts. If Matthew were written before 85 we might think of it as a kind of dialogue with the synagogue authorities and communities, albeit a fairly forthright one. If it were written after 85, then it could be regarded as having a harder tone, both affirming the converts in their decisions, and providing practical resources for the development of the new religion. Commentators generally opt for a date around 85, and views can be found at all points on the scale indicated above.

If we are to think about identifying with this group and their context we have therefore to think of situations which are characterized by changes of identity, and by the anxiety that usually attends fundamental decisions involving change. We have already seen how the author wants to see this as a significant moment in the history of the world: the threshold of a new age. It is therefore to be expected that this is projected as a time of confusion and chaos, that calls for decisiveness. We shall see as we progress that Matthew relies on the apocalyptic tradition as his commentary on this confused situation, and as a way of understanding anxiety. We might also expect some discussion about the religious life. To be a devout Jew was to adhere to the law and to regard it as the means of salvation, so we might expect discussion and debate about both the status of the law in the new religion and also what Christian life looks like, and how it differs from a law-based approach. On identity we might also expect discussion around whether only Jews can become Christians. There are surely bound to

be questions around how this new religion is organized. What does the new community of faith look
like and how is it ministered to?

We shall find all these as major themes in the
Gospel.

To do

Look back at the initial paragraphs of this chapter and the proposed 'modern' themes that the
Gospel might address. Having started to read
Matthew, do those scenarios seem more or less
likely, or more or less interesting to you? Do you
think Chris is likely to be helped by the approach
set out here?

2

Jesus the Radical

TJ is an apprentice in an automotive factory. He is a quick learner and is enjoying both his time at the factory and his day at the College of Further Education each week. One unforeseen consequence has been the awakening of an interest in politics, both from the perspective of his trade union membership, and his attendance at a Student Political Society. Both these have found him at a protest march against social inequality. He is surprised to find that alongside him are not only political activists and trade unionists, but also some young members of a local church. These were the very people he expected to be wedded to the status quo. And he is curious. He wants to know where these people find their inspiration, and how it can be that young Christians can also want to be engaged in political and social change. One member of the church group tells him that actually, Jesus himself was a radical. He wants to know: was she right?

To do

Think about what the word 'radical' means in your experience. Can you think of a person that you would describe as a radical, and what makes that person a radical. It might be that a political figure springs to mind, but, alternatively, it may be that someone has been responsible for a radical overhaul of your business. Perhaps a new headmaster has radically altered the ethos of a school, or a new CEO has radically restructured a company. The word 'radical' comes from the Greek word for 'root'. Is that a helpful way of considering what different kinds of radical have in common? As a result of your thinking, what kind of evidence might you be looking for to decide about whether Jesus was a radical? It might be good to come back to this question at the end of the chapter.

We have already seen in the first two chapters of his Gospel that while Matthew has been keen to emphasize continuity, that is not the whole story. Yes, Jesus stands in a tradition. He has a genealogy that connects him with significant figures in Jewish religion, imagination and expectation. But as we move on we see that Matthew does not simply want to present Jesus as a reforming Jew. Alongside the continuity that gives some categories for determining who exactly Jesus is, there is a critical dissonance that undermines some of the securities that characterized Jewish religious life. We see, first, the boast that 'We have Abraham as our father' being rubbished by John the Baptist (3.9). His invective is directed particularly towards the religious functionaries (3.7–10). He calls them a vipers' brood – a term echoed later by Jesus himself (12.34, 23.33). But at a different level, Jews regarded keeping the Torah as their guarantee of being right with God. In the first great sermon or discourse of the five identified in the Gospel, Jesus examines this claim, and while saying that he did not come to abolish the law but to fulfil it (5.17), he offers some radically different understandings of what a truly religious life looks like. In the process he also challenges the security offered by those who are familiar and comfortable with the liturgy and who believe that maintaining a liturgical life is sufficient to claim God's favour. Not everyone who can say 'Lord, Lord' will enter the kingdom of Heaven (7.21–2). Between the Baptism and the Sermon, we have a much fuller account of the Temptation of Jesus than appears in Mark, in which Jesus refuses to accept some of the expectations that traditional Judaism have placed on their Messiah. These are radical claims, challenging the conservatism of the religious establishment.

But there is perhaps even a more radical challenge than that – a challenge to what is generally regarded as religion. In most religions the aim is for humans to get right with God by doing the right things and performing the right rituals. Particular ethnic groups may be privileged within this scheme. It is a hierarchical scheme that needs functionaries, inter-preters and people who claim to know God better than most. Quite sophisticated religious systems can be built around this basic set of ideas. All of that is being challenged at the outset by Matthew. His claim, the basic Christian claim, is that the ini-tiative in this process of what we might call salva-tion does not rest with humans but with God. Jesus is God's reaching out towards humankind. As one famous Reformer said, it is his act of making friends with us. There is nothing we can do, and nothing God wants us to do, that will catch his attention in a way that gives us an advantage over the next per-son. This is what Paul describes in terms of 'Grace'. Salvation is God's gift without religious strings attached.

Matthew uses two traditions to structure his argument. On the one hand he wants to refer back to the Old Covenant of the Old Testament, and to claim that it has been subverted by the religious establishment. What was an intensely relational agreement between God and humankind has been reduced to a set of institutional rules, mediated by a set of self-appointed and unworthy gatekeepers. He wants to speak of a *new* covenant community. On the other, he wants to present a dynamic picture of the Kingdom of Heaven. For Matthew, what is at stake is entry into that Kingdom, to be a citi-zen under God's kingly rule. And he is clear that no religious system or ethnic identity confers privilege in that. This is not just a continuity. Something new is here. In the three accounts of Baptism, Temptation and Sermon, we see this agenda being pursued.

Read Matthew 3

We see here, first of all, an emphasis on the Kingdom. Unlike Luke and Mark, Matthew connects Jesus with John's proclamation of the Kingdom (4.17). We shall have a chance to look at Jewish religious expectation in more detail in later passages, but it is important from the outset to realize that inclusion in the Kingdom is basically what is at stake for religious people in the Jewish tradition. Hugely disappointed political hopes, allied with a community life which was precarious and open to all kinds of corruption and abuse, had led religious Jews to search the scriptures to see how creation and redemption could have gone so sour, and how God's promises might be given real effect. From Old Testament prophecies and further later reflections upon them, the expectation had arisen for a new phase in the history of the world, in which the obvious faults of the present, in personal, communal and even cosmic terms, could be repaired. They had only the vocabulary of the Old Testament to describe this new state of affairs and so they called it the Kingdom of God (or Heaven, if you didn't want to utter the name of God, as a good Jew), and that was what everyone wanted to be part of. There were three questions about it. One was how would it be inaugurated; another was who could become citizens of it; and finally, what would life be like within it. Within this understanding, there was a special role for one who would be a new anointed (Hebrew: messiah) servant or son of God. We see in these early chapters those titles ascribed to Jesus.

The second clue from chapter 3 is that Jesus is essentially taking on the religious establishment of his day. Unlike Luke (Luke 3.7–14), Matthew specifically targets the Pharisees and Sadducees. Luke's message is a more universal one and the examples he gives of repentance cover a variety of professions. For Matthew, it is religious practice that must change. The Sadducees and Pharisees form a target group for Matthew. Matthew mentions Sadducees six times, Mark and Luke only once. His is the only Gospel that consistently groups and criticizes them (see for example Matthew 16.1, 6, 11, 12). The Sadducees were the aristocrats of the priestly caste, who ran the Temple. Interested in religious politics and power, they had gained wealth and position. A further grouping is scribes and Pharisees, again representative of the old privileged order (see for example Matthew 23.2, 13, 15, 23, 25, 27, 29).

Matthew's account of the Temptation of Jesus is a greatly expanded version of what appears in Mark and is similar to the account in Luke. This forms part of the material that scholars call 'Q'. This is material common to Matthew and Luke, possibly written, possibly oral, but nevertheless a distinguishable and separate source for the Gospels.

Read Matthew 4.1–11

To do

Consider the following scenario:

Patrick was a bright boy. Everyone said he had a great potential. He shone in primary school, excelled in secondary school and had a stellar career in university. Everyone said that the world was his oyster. When it came to considering what he should do next, he did not lack advice. His family wanted him to work in the city where he would be sure to make a lot of money, afford a great lifestyle and have a lovely home. Friends suggested that international travel would be a great incentive to join a global business empire. Others pointed out that rich good-looking young men had no difficulty in attracting desirable young women. Patrick was his own man however, and he realized that what he had gained, apart from qualifications, was actually the power to choose. As a practising Roman Catholic, he decided that he would speak to his priest about his options. The priest recommended that he read Matthew 4.1–11 and reflect on it before deciding his next moves. Eventually,

Patrick took a management job in the charity
sector.

- How do you think reading the Bible passage
  might have influenced Patrick?
- Does his story shed any new perspective on
  the Temptation of Jesus for you?
- Is there a sense in which Patrick's choice
  could have been described as 'radical'?

The first thing we notice about the Temptation of
Jesus is that his is not the kind of temptation we
face ourselves. He is not tempted to lie, cheat, steal
or have an illicit affair. In other words, he is not
being tempted here as a human being, but rather as
the tempter says, he is being tempted as the Son of
God. It is important to see the passage as related to
the Baptism passage that precedes it. Both give us
insight into what it will mean to be Jesus, Son of
God. Immediately before the Temptation account,
at the conclusion of the Baptism, we have heard
the voice from heaven saying, 'This is my beloved
son in whom I take delight' (3.17). This is the only
public declaration of Sonship that we read at this
point in the Gospels. Both Mark and Luke use the
second person: 'You are my Son . . .' etc. There are
allusions in this statement that would be recognized
by the audience. Psalm 2.7 reads, 'You are my son,
today I have begotten you.' Isaiah 42.1 reads, 'Here
is my servant whom I uphold, my chosen in whom
my soul delights.' Together with the setting at the

Jordan, which Israel crossed to take possession of the land, in the tradition, and the following reference to 'forty', an idiom used of Israel as well as other Old Testament figures to describe a time of reflecting on vocation, that statement from heaven conveys more than it might seem to us. This is then expanded in the Temptation accounts. Hagner sums up the combined effect thus: 'we encounter a theme that is vital in the theology of the Gospels. The goal of obedience to the Father is accomplished, not by triumphant self-assertion, not by the exercise of power and authority, but paradoxically by the way of humility, service and suffering' (Hagner 1993, vol. 1, p. 70). This could be described as a radical departure from what most people expected of religious figures.

To do

Consider the case of Brian. He is a former Christian and now one of religion's fiercest critics. He describes Christianity as a rule-bound and conservative institution, little better in its ritual than pagan superstition, all policed by holier-than-thou functionaries largely remote from the issues and problems of ordinary life. You may know people like him. Often some particular rule of the institutional Church has led to a feeling of being an outsider and so prompted their view – in Brian's case, he is gay. He has friends who were refused marriage in church because they were divorced.

As you read through the next sections of the Gospel, which consist of Jesus speaking to people, imagine him speaking to Brian and his friends. How do you think they might react?

There is a problem for early Christians who want to establish its distinctiveness: to distinguish their new view of God from religion as it was then understood and practised. There is a world view, a behaviour and way of life that follows from this new Christian belief that looks very much like law. And there is a way of worshipping together as Christians that looks very much like old fashioned ritual and sacrifice. And there is a form of Christian ministry that looks very much like the systems of priests, scribes and Pharisees. So how is the difference to be described?

The first of the five identified discourses sits within what may be two sets of brackets. The one suggested by Kingsbury (1975) (see Chapter 1) would see 4.17 and 16.21, with their repeated, 'from that time', as the outermost brackets. The material between these brackets constitutes, for him, Jesus's public ministry. A further set of brackets is the repeated descriptions of 4.23 and 9.35. These describe the nature and priorities of Jesus's ministry in Galilee: teaching, proclaiming and healing. Some commentators again notice the priority of teaching, and compare that with Jesus's final commission to his disciples to teach in 28.20. The 'tightest' set of brackets is the opening of the discourse itself at 5.1, and the sign-off, repeated at the end of each discourse, 'When Jesus had finished . . .' (7.28). It opens with the beatitudes. The remainder of chapter 5 is a series of references to the law, each introduced by a formula: 'you have heard that it was said . . . but I say to you', each offering a new insight into laws which had lost any sense of relationship with righteousness. Chapter 6 deals with religious observance (vv 1–18), and with our attitude towards life. Chapter 7 is essentially about relationships between humans, and between humankind and God.

Read Matthew 5.1–20

This is one of the best-known passages in the whole of the New Testament. Luke has a similar list (Luke 6.20–6), also contained within a much shorter 'sermon' or address. In Matthew's first discourse about half the material is peculiar to him, and about half shared with Luke, who does not group it all in the same way. There is some scholarly discussion about which account is the more original. Luke contains his beatitudes with woes against the rich, well-fed and content, so giving the beatitudes a more general social context. For Matthew these are the first contribution he makes to one of the questions of the day: what will the Kingdom of Heaven be like?

In this poetic passage, Matthew records what is a consistent message throughout the Gospels, that the Kingdom will be a surprise, especially to those who benefit from the status quo, and will involve a complete reversal of values and perceptions. The first will be last, the least will be greatest (Matthew 18.2–3).

There are some subtleties of language that we need to be aware of if we read the beatitudes in English translation. There are two words in Greek for 'blessed'. One is the Greek word *makarios*, the other is *eulogeo*. This latter translates the Hebrew *beraka*, and is the word used in any liturgical sense, such as 'the blessing of God be upon you'. *Makarios* has the more objective sense of 'how fortunate'. The fact that *makarios* is used here completely changes the sense that many people have of this passage. It is not saying, if you do X you will receive Y. It is observing that some categories of people experience blessedness as a present reality and because of that, a future hope. Kenneth Bailey describes this relationship between present and future with the example of the daughter of a farmer, Farmer Jones, who will inherit a farm. 'The woman in question is already the happy daughter of Mr Jones. She is not working to earn the farm. Everyone knows that a key element in her happy and secure life is that she and the community around her know that the farm will one day be hers' (Bailey 2008, p. 68). The radical claim here is that the poor in spirit, those who mourn and who recognize God's comfort, the meek, and so on, already enjoy the Kingdom. They are examples of a new kind of human experience and aspiration.

Another example of translation nuance is to be found at 7.28, where some translations (e.g. REB) tell us that 'the people were amazed at his teaching'. The Greek word translated 'people' is in fact the word 'crowds', the same word we find at 5.1. For some commentators, defining the *audience* for Jesus's sayings is important (Fenton 1963, p. 76; France 1985, p. 113). Jesus addresses the *disciples*, and distances himself from the *crowds* (5.1), who apparently still had access to his words. This puzzle is normally solved by locating the disciples as the teachers of the crowds. 'Although he addressed his disciples, he was training them for later leadership of the crowds' (Minear 1984, p. 46).

The beatitudes are followed by a key passage. What is Jesus's attitude to the Old Testament law? The passage that follows 5.20 is peculiar to Matthew and deals with interpretation of the law. Throughout the Gospel, controversies in which Jesus engages with opponents are often about the interpretation of the law (see for example 12.1–8, 9–14, 15.1–20, 17.24–7, 19.3–9). He is prepared to alter source material from Mark to present Jesus as a controversial figure. Mark 12.28–34 shows Jesus in creative conversation with a scribe who clearly admires him and agrees with some of what he has said. Matthew 22.34–40 puts the question about the law on the lips of one of the Sadducees and Pharisees, as a deliberate attempt to catch him out. The issue here is that devout Jews treated every article of the law as having equal validity. Jesus sets the love commandments as the greatest, and as the ones in the light of which the others should be understood.

There has been much scholarly discussion on this subject. Some of that has focused on how to understand the word 'fulfil' in 5.17. A scale of possibilities ranging from 'supersede' or 'replace' to 'confirm', 'validate', or 'extend and amplify' appears to be possible. The main problem, though, is that Matthew appears ambivalent. On the one hand Jesus seems to be downgrading the law. On the other hand he abhors lawlessness. This is not always apparent in English translations. The Greek word *anomia*, lawlessness, is often translated as 'evil doers' at 7.23 and 13.41. This is the same word that is used at 24.12, where lawlessness is generally used to translate it. It is perhaps notable that in that passage the lawlessness is associated with a love grown cold.

Scholarly solutions to the problem of ambivalence include the possibility that Matthew had two audiences in mind in his mixed Christian community of Jews and Gentiles. One might have too rigorous a view of law and the other too liberal a view, or indeed, if they were to be associated, as some scholars believe, with a Pauline faction, a view which saw law as having been replaced with grace. The classic statement of this view is that of Gerhard Barth in his extended essay in *Tradition and Interpretation in Matthew* (Bornkamm, Barth and Held 1963). Others have suggested that Matthew used different layers of tradition, though it seems unlikely that he would willingly include traditional elements that ran counter to his main thesis. These kinds of interpretation relate to the predominant critical methods of their times: form and redaction criticism both of which encourage scholars to look at the way a final edition is formed, by charting the ways in which small units of tradition are conveyed to, and used by, the authors. More recent work has seen the Gospel as a literary whole. Scholars have interpreted 5.17 as a Christological statement. In other words, it is a way of describing the significance of Jesus, using traditional religious categories that would help us to know how to place him within their own understanding about who God is and how he has worked. This statement is about the authority of Jesus. The idea that Jesus is simply presented as a second Moses delivering a new law for Christians (Bacon 1930) has not been widely accepted, though as France concedes, elsewhere in the Gospel there is evidence that the relationship between Jesus and Moses had traction (France 1985, p. 112).

Read Matthew 5.21–6

What we see here is Jesus giving an intelligent and nuanced commentary on an issue which when treated simply by religious people as 'a law to be observed' could be overlooked. For example, it is commonplace nowadays in Middle Eastern or Peace Studies to look at the causes of spiralling violence, and to see combinations of lack of knowledge/ignorance, fear, anger and hatred leading to violence. Christians today in the Middle East and elsewhere are being urged to recognize those causes and to deal with them before they result in violence. Christians sing hymns with words like 'Let there be peace on earth and let it begin with me', acknowledging that there is a link between personal behaviour and attitudes that affect world peace. Perhaps this experience of being members of such churches gives us some insight into Jesus's intention that more remote scholars may have missed. In terms of hyperbole, Jesus is encouraging Christians to understand what lies behind the law, and what a complete keeping of it involves. This is surely the better righteousness that 5.20 urges. That relates both to Jesus's authority as the ultimate teacher, and to his insistence on the primacy of love. In other words, we see here both continuity with the past understanding of the law and something new.

There has been much scholarly discussion about how we are to regard the ethical demands of the Sermon on the Mount, and to what extent they are normative for Christians. While we have become adept at defining the ten commandments in ways that enable them to sit beside modern ordinary life, the Sermon on the Mount is less adaptable.

Robin Gill speaks about the dilemma they pose for the modern business community, for example. 'If they were to follow the injunctions of the Sermon on the Mount literally, their business would probably collapse' (Gill 2006, p. 141). Case-Winters describes the ways in which scholars have tried to rescue the ethical teaching contained here from the charge of being unrealistic. One is to regard them as being requirements only for a set period, immediately before a supposed second coming for example. Thus, they can be regarded as an 'interim-ethic'. Or they can be regarded as applying only to a limited company of people, clergy perhaps, or even just the disciples. Or they can be regarded as *reductio ad absurdum* case studies demonstrating the impossibility of the law being kept and hence the futility of trying to do so. As she points out, each of these limits the ethical demand substantially. She concludes, 'I would propose that the ethic of the Sermon on the Mount is a fitting ethic, not just for "the interim" and not just for the inner circle but for followers of Jesus in all times and places . . . a new way of life is at the heart of the gospel call' (Case-Winters 2015, p. 71).

Read Matthew 5.43–8

Can you find examples from your experience today, in churches or elsewhere, that confirm the interpretation that Jesus gives? Stanton

---

describes vv 43 and 44 as 'one of the most radical and demanding of the sayings of Jesus, a saying that sums up the ethos of the Sermon as a whole and is as relevant today as it was in the first century' (Stanton 1992, p. 744). Do you agree? Do you think that our original questioner TJ would agree? What effect do you think this might have on his idea of political protest?

Perhaps, then, what 'fulfil' comes to mean is a deeper interpretation of the law, related to examples which the audience might recognize from their experience. To some extent these are radical in that they are counter-cultural. But the point is surely that the original intention has been obscured by cultural overlay. A further point is worth making, namely that for Jews the keeping of the law was the route to salvation and membership of the new Kingdom. For Matthew, Jesus is the new authority. Understanding the demands of the law as he has set them out, and adopting behaviour and a world view consistent with them, is the new norm.

To do

Think for a moment about the way humans mature. As children we are taught rules and boundaries. The key question we ask is, 'Am I allowed?' We are taught not to question. As adolescents we do question, sometimes rebel, but as more mature and formed humans we come to realize the sophistication of what we had once just regarded as an obligation, and experience confirms the value of what we had once questioned. Do you see any of this kind of development in Jesus's restatement of the law in chapter 5?

Chapter 6 consists almost entirely of material not to be found elsewhere. It is particularly Matthean, and is consistent with his clear belief that the religious system has become corrupted. In the kind of religious system in which the aim is for humans to do the right things and perform the right rituals to maintain safe life, there is an inevitable culture of anxiety. And if there are identified gatekeepers and interpreters built into the system, there is clear opportunity for them to exercise power and abuse authority in a way that feeds that anxiety and boosts the importance of the functionaries. That appears to be Matthew's case against the Pharisees and Sadducees. What Jesus does, in his teaching in this Gospel, is to get back to the roots of piety and devotion. He offers a radical critique of current practice. It is sometimes said that the warning against parading religion in 6.1 is at odds with the encouragement to 'let your light shine before men' in 5.16. The two cases are entirely different. There is all the difference in the world between living out a Christian life so attractive that others may want to be part of it, on the one hand, and thrusting your religious principles in people's faces in a most unattractive way, on the other.

To do

Do you agree with this distinction? Can you think of examples of both attractive and unattractive public expressions of religious faith?

Chapter 6 includes Matthew's version of the Lord's Prayer. It is different from that of Luke and comes at a completely different place in the ministry of Jesus (cf. Luke 11.1–4). It may be that these are accounts of two separate events (so France 1985, p. 137), but in any case there is a marked difference of atmosphere in Matthew's version. The current scholarly debate is about the extent to which the prayer refers exclusively to the Kingdom. Each petition may be interpreted in that way. What is certain is that this is a prayer for disciples in the widest sense.

It is in chapter 6 that we come across what Fenton describes as one of the difficulties he supposes for the modern reader, and that is the question of rewards and punishments. The question becomes acute, when, as in chapter 6, rewards and punishments appear to be presented as motives for action (Fenton 1963, p. 24). Generations of Christians have been brought up on the prayer that 'we seek no reward save that of knowing that we do thy will', so is chapter 6 an embarrassment in that respect?

We must take account of Matthew's preference for apocalyptic language, already noted, which deals in hyperbole, and does in fact promise to save good men from evil, thereby requiring detailed descriptions of the two alternatives. But given that, Fenton has three possible responses. One is that Christianity never pretends to be disinterested. 'It offers salvation to people as something that is to their advantage.' Second, it is a general New Testament theme that 'God's rewards are always greater than men's deserts.' Third, the reward that is promised is of a life which ironically is one of 'self-forgetfulness and abandonment to God' (pp. 25–6). Case-Winters believes there is a more sophisticated sub-text to discover in connection with the power of grace and the obligation to righteousness. Matthew is the only one of the first three Gospel writers to use the word 'righteousness'. 'The "righteousness" to which the Sermon on the Mount calls people is not a sinless perfection, but a calling to do justice and love mercy' (Case-Winters 2015, p. 76).

To do

Look at chapter 6 with the question about rewards in mind. You might like to compare some other passages in Matthew which concentrate on punishments: 13.42, 22.13, 24.51, 25.30. Are you convinced by Fenton's arguments? Have you got a better solution?

The Sermon on the Mount concludes with observations about anxiety, which can be construed as exhortations to faith. The climax and summary of what has gone before comes in 7.12. This version of the so-called golden rule is unusual in that it is expressed positively rather than negatively, but it is by no means unique. What makes it unique in this context is Jesus's linking it to the detailed commentary he has already given on the attitudes of the Christian life. In the remainder of chapter 7, the verb 'to do' is dominant, reinforcing the demand that the Christian life is to be lived out and not just treated as theoretically desirable.

In the developing story about Jesus we have seen how religious life has been reinterpreted. Key words here are Messiah, Kingdom and discipleship. Jesus has been identified as the servant Messiah in whom God delights. His proclamation begins with the announcement of the Kingdom, in the messianic tradition, and all that follows relates to these themes. He calls disciples whom he teaches to instruct other disciples, members of the new religious community, and does so with authority. The question for religious people is no longer: what does the law say, how do you read? Now it is: what are the demands of discipleship and what must I do? What does life as a disciple of Jesus look like? Am I already blessed in the life of the Kingdom?

To do

So, do you think TJ might be convinced or Brian persuaded? Have your own conditions for 'radical' been met?

3

Jesus and his Followers

In the office where she works, Nikki is often accused by older colleagues as 'living on her phone'. Nikki just thinks the rest are dinosaurs. For her, the phone is not a toy, as they seem to imagine, but rather an important way in which she relates to the world. She gets much of the information that helps form her opinions from her phone. Through social media she feels part of several communities who 'like' the same things and ideas. Her Twitter account shows that she is a follower. She follows a number of well-known opinion formers as well as celebrities and a quirky stand-up comic. If called upon to defend her use of her phone she says that it is far more democratic, subversive even, than older people's ways of accepting what the newspapers tell them and believing what politicians or religious leaders say without question. Recently she has been troubled by reports that social media can also be manipulated and fake news can even help win elections. One older trusted colleague, Mary, is a church-goer and in discussion with her, Nikki has found a different take on issues around truth, authority and being a follower. She has agreed to go along to a Bible study series which is looking at the Gospel of Matthew at Mary's house. She wants to see where Mary's view comes from, and whether it is possible to make sense of it in her twenty-first-century world.

To do

Think for a moment about Nikki. Do you recognize her in yourself or someone else? What do you think is involved in being a 'follower' in her sense? What do you think the main differences might be between her idea of authority and those of her older colleagues? Where do you stand on that spectrum?

Mary has explained that Nikki is joining the group a couple of weeks in, and that some of the themes around authority and truth have already been introduced. Today they are beginning at chapter 8, but the following section of the Gospel has quite a lot to say about the issues that particularly interest Nikki.

The last verse of chapter 7 gives a summary of the response to Jesus's mountain teaching. 'Unlike their scribes, he taught with a note of authority.' That note is reinforced as we then read that Jesus comes down from the mountain, just as Moses did (8.1). As we have seen, Matthew is not very interested in an arresting continuous narrative, complete with picturesque detail, such as Mark provides. He deals with his subject, rather, in a thematic way, placing set pieces of various kinds in a way that allows each to build on the insights of its predecessor. These linking and introductory verses suggest that one theme we might expect in the next section is authority. For Case-Winters it is actually the main theme (Case-Winters 2015, p. 123).

There is a real link here with Nikki's questions about authority, in that the status quo in Jesus's time was an authority structure based on national culture and religion that has already come under fierce criticism. We have to remember that the main area of Jesus's ministry was part of what sociologists call an Agrarian empire. 'Agrarian empires are marked by a very steep hierarchy and great inequality with control and wealth in the hands of a very few' (Saldarini 1988, p. 36). The two classes of governors and peasants are separated by a wide gulf, and the peasants struggle with excessive taxes (up to 70 per cent of the crop). This can only work by the exercise of power through force on the one hand, and by an appeal to commitment to Jewish identity on the other. Jesus's authority is legitimized in a different way: not by appointment or rank, but rather by the acclamation of the people. His followers are followers precisely because they accept this different kind of authority.

Something we have not yet remarked on is that, unlike Luke, who arranges his material in two volumes: one dealing with the time of Jesus, and one dealing with the age of the Church, Matthew has only one volume, but is nevertheless very interested in the Church. His solution is to superimpose the story of the Church on the story of Jesus. This invites the reader to see the Gospel material in two ways. On the one hand, we can see how authority works in the time of Jesus and how he attracts disciples, followers, who trust him and accept his authority. On the other, it gives insight into the Church as the later community of followers in all ages, and how authority works there too.

This interest of Matthew's then becomes related to the nature of the Church itself, and this relates to Nikki's interest in followers. Who can be disciples, if being a follower is not based on race or lineage, and what do these disciples do? Those questions are brought together particularly well at 9.8: 'the people were filled with awe at the sight and praised God for granting such authority to human beings [lit. men]'. The actions which prompt this awe are acts of healing, and the authority described is not restricted to Jesus. The next section of the Gospel deals with these themes.

From the beginning of chapter 8 we see first a collection of miracles. Like the material in the Sermon on the Mount, these accounts are distributed more widely in Luke and Mark but are brought together here. The second is another discourse; the second in the series of five, in which Jesus deals with questions around apostleship. What does it mean when a disciple, a follower and learner, becomes an apostle, one who is sent to teach and heal? How is Jesus's authority maintained in his followers?

At one level we can read this in a way which sets the context entirely in the time of Jesus. As such we see that insights from the previous chapters are exemplified and further emphasized. So Jesus is the figure of authority. He can do what it was reckoned only God could do (9.3). He exercises control over what people generally thought could not be controlled: the weather and the madness of mental illness (8.27, 9.33). He is the one who has not come to abolish the law, but, for example, to see it observed in the directions he gives to the leper who is healed (8.4). His behaviour is surprising and counter-cultural. He is the Messiah of action, showing that mercy is the important thing rather than ritual observance (9.13), making a priority of healing as well as teaching. He continues to proclaim the Kingdom (9.35), giving further examples of what Kingdom life is like. He is not afraid to enter alien places, inhabited by Gentiles (8.28).

To do

Matthew's priority has been to put teaching before action. Do you agree with this priority? In a Christian minister, do you look for teaching and preaching ability first, or pastoral sensitivity? What are the pros and cons of both options?

What Matthew does not seem to be doing is direct-
ing our attention in an undivided way to Jesus
the miracle worker. The fact that what he does is
miraculous is almost incidental to his main themes.
Fenton believes that interpretation of the miracles is
one of the barriers to fully engaging with Matthew
(Fenton 1963, pp. 19ff). His solution is to see
miracle stories as a late accretion to genuine tradition about Jesus. He points to evidence that traditions attract more miracle stories the more they
develop. He would be right to say that Matthew's
concern is not to present Jesus simply as a miracle
worker, and indeed Fenton's concern could be better illustrated in other Gospels. In any case that is
not sufficient reason to suspect the veracity of the
miracle tradition as a whole. On the other hand,
each of these stories does describe a kind of miracle
beyond straightforward medical concerns. Healing
has implications. The story of the Good Samaritan,
peculiar to Luke, is, in a sense, describing something as miraculous and incredible as the curing of
disease, and to see these as all of a piece is surely
something of a literary triumph. Certainly, in this
section, we are also encouraged by incidental references to the cost of discipleship, to read these
accounts as describing the responsibilities of church
membership: of the importance of faith in difficult
times. We are encouraged to see the Church following its pioneer into Gentile areas. We are given
examples of boundary-crossing activity. We are
given pictures of the Church with which to conjure:

fishers, harvesters, sailors, shepherds. The section culminates in the discourse about apostleship.

Read chapters 8 and 9. How many times do you find a reference to following? See if you can find the references to the pictures of the Church and its ministry mentioned above. What would it mean to apply each of them to church life today? What would a church of fishers look like, or a church of harvesters? Which picture do you think has most contemporary relevance? Thinking back over the earlier chapters are there other pictures describing discipleship that you find particularly striking?

Matthew has stripped of all but their most basic structure the miracles that he has adopted from Mark. His aim is not to tell a story but to stack up examples and exemplars. So we have ten miracle stories. The fact that after Jesus comes down from the mountain we are immediately confronted with ten of anything is interesting, and it invites comparison with Moses and the ten commandments. The ten miracles from chapters 8 and 9 are arranged in three groups of three (one occasion involves two healings). The twin artificiality of the arrangement and the abridgement prompts suspicion of ulterior motives and secondary messages and presentation strategies. So, while it is not denied that Jesus healed the sick – that is, after all, a common theme in the Gospels – it becomes clear that 'healing' for Matthew means more than making sick people better. Perhaps the whole passage is best read in the light of 9.12: 'It is not the healthy who need a doctor, but the sick', where 'the sick' refers to those with whom Jesus ate and drank who were considered inappropriate company for him. The first group of three presents controversial candidates for healing. The first is someone with a skin disease, rendering him unclean (Leviticus 13.1–39; the term 'leper' is used to refer to a wide variety of such conditions). The second is a centurion, and therefore a Gentile, but even worse, a member of the occupying forces. The third is a woman. Healing these three in the presence now of 'the crowds' and not just the disciples has several effects. It demonstrates Jesus's willingness to cross borders of convention and prejudice. It reinforces the Matthean message that there is no privilege for the religious Jews, and it is inclusive, in that it brings the afflicted back into mainstream society. These are also messages for the followers of the future.

It is a constant theme throughout the whole section that Jesus's healing is a response to faith. Each of the people, unlikely as it seems, recognize Jesus for who he is, and believe that he has the power to help them. They also display humility in his presence by kneeling before him in some instances (8.2, 9.18) and addressing him as *Kyrios* in others (8.6). This is contrasted with the scribes in 9.3, who dispute his authority.

This conflict presents 'faith' as a subversive category challenging the grounds on which the authorities base their own authority. This passage of Matthew bears some relation to the kind of message that is more commonly associated with Luke, in passages such as the Good Samaritan story (Luke 10.25–37). That was told in illustration of Jesus's interpretation of the most important law, and these miracles follow an extended reflection on the law that includes the golden rule (7.12). Jesus here demonstrates compassion. That point is emphasized in the conclusion at 9.36. Minear is probably too restrictive in describing this passage as a model for Christian physicians to follow (Minear 1984). This looks more like the expression of Christian ministry more generally. This is the attractive exercise of Christian faith which is reflected at 5.16: 'Let your light so shine before men that they may see your good works and give glory to your father who is in heaven.' Case-Winters (2015) describes its modern application thus:

> Oppression, exploitation, and human rights violations are all over the news. Corrupt politicians supported by systems of 'law and order' that are without transparency or accountability constitute authority in many locations. Suspicion of such authorities is well justified. But what if there was a different kind of authority, a different kind of power? Jesus demonstrates an altogether different kind of authority. It has nothing to do with violence and violations. It is the power to help and

to heal, to show mercy and justice/righteousness.
(p. 125)

To do

- How do you think Nikki would react to the
  quotation above?
- Now read the account of the stilling of the
  storm in Matthew 8.23–7, and then compare
  it with the way Mark uses the same tradition
  (Mark 4.35–41). What differences can you
  see? How might you account for them?

The second set of three miracles is preceded by a
short section (8.23–7) about the difficulty of discipleship, which gives a context for what follows.

You may notice the following. There is no specific
context for Mark's account, whereas for Matthew
the verb 'to follow' offers a clear link. Indeed, making the link seems to be the only function of the preceding passage which otherwise simply interrupts
the flow. This miracle story is going to be about
following. The next difference will be most obvious
to those who read the Greek text. The word that
Mark uses for 'storm' is the kind of word meteorol-
ogists might use. Its meaning is, literally, wind. The
word that Matthew uses is *seismos*, the word that
gives us the English word for the study of earth-
quakes. This is an earth-shattering event. It is paralleled at 28.2 where it introduces a post-resurrection

appearance. Its use here suggests something similar. The words that the disciples use in Mark's account really make them sound like men afraid for their lives. Matthew's disciples use words reminiscent of liturgy. In Mark, Jesus stills the storm and then addresses the disciples. In Matthew he speaks of little faith in the midst of the storm. All of this, in Matthew, is confirmed by the crowds (literally 'men'). The suggestion is (Bornkamm 1963) that what we have here is a story about the Church. It serves to remind would-be disciples that the way may well be hard and that much faith will be required. Thus the theme of faith saving people is continued with a new slant. It was the faith of those healed that saved them. Jesus will respond to the faith of disciples in stormy times for the Church.

The next miracle, which is hugely abbreviated from its Markan form (Mark 5.1–20), can be read as a continuation of both themes. On the one hand, the demons recognize Jesus for who he is. They acknowledge his authority. On the other, the Church must venture into Gentile areas. They can be dangerous or at least scary, but Jesus has cleared the way. Gentile demons have been dispatched in a particularly Gentile way, in pigs. If we could imagine ourselves reading this account as former religious Jews, we might say that they were hoist by their own petard. We seem to be invited to read the miracles in this section in this dual way. Matthew's abbreviation has taken away the narratives about symptoms and methods of cure. It has played down the wonder-working aspect of the stories. It has concentrated instead on the outcomes, and particularly the words of Jesus and the crowds. These have the effect of shifting the emphasis from straightforward power (Mark) to authority (Matthew). It is notable that, in 10.1, it is authority that Jesus gives to his disciples, as they continue his mission. They also maintain the strand of these being Jesus's deeds that mirror his words. The final words of the section, or the first words of the next section (11.1), emphasize this in case we've missed it.

The third cycle of miracles is preceded by, first, the call of Matthew, and then by a couple of disputes, first with the Pharisees and then with the disciples of John. Hare characterizes these as 'The Right to Associate with Sinners' and 'The Right to be Joyful' (Hare 1993, pp. 101ff). Matthew clearly anticipates that some of his readers, and indeed some of the Gospel characters, will be scandalized (see Jesus's response at 11.5). The shocking elements are that forgiveness is offered without repentance or confession; that Jesus calls a tax collector, and that he associates with both tax collectors and 'other' sinners. The story of Zacchaeus (Luke 19.1–10) shows how tax collectors were viewed, and in his promise to repay what he has defrauded people of, we see the reason for popular suspicion. Whereas the story of Zacchaeus is well known, the call of Matthew is, if anything, even more explosively controversial. Including these controversial actions of Jesus in this section of his ministry suggests that these actions of

his are as germane to his Messiahship as are healings and exorcisms. They are also to be, by exten-
sion, a characteristic of the Church founded on the
authority given to followers.

There may also be an intended link with 10.6, and
the mission to 'lost sheep'. The climax is the saying of
Jesus that new wine needs new skins. In other words,
there is incompatibility between the old and the new.
The emphasis at 9.17, that by putting new wine into
new skins rather than old, *both are preserved* – that
is, both the old and the new – may indicate that for
Matthew both the old and the new have value, and
the new cannot be manipulated to fit the categories
and expectations and limitations of the old.

To do

At 9.14 we see an 'internal' discussion between
the followers of John and those of Jesus that
leads to the wine skins illustration. Douglas
Hare writes, 'John the Baptist has many followers among modern Christians. We often brood
gloomily over the evils of the world, instead of
searching out and celebrating what God is doing
in our midst' (Hare 1993, p. 105). Is this true in
your experience? Can you think of other kinds of
example of people trying to interpret a dynamic
Jesus with the categories provided by historic
religion? Is this possible? When have the wine-
skins burst?

According to the classic study by H. J. Held, the theme of the final group of three miracles is 'praying faith' (Bornkamm, Barth and Held 1963, pp. 165–299). As we have seen, faith has been an important motif in the previous two cycles also. This section ratifies and confirms that. It maintains the theme that the faith of those who need healing is strong (9.2, 18, 20, 28). There is a further summary at 11.5, where Jesus tells John's disciples to report both what they have heard, and what they have seen. What they have seen is described as 'the blind recover their sight, the lame walk, lepers are made clean, the deaf hear, the dead are raised to life, the poor are brought good news, and blessed are those who do not find me an obstacle to faith' (literally: who are not scandalized by me; 11.5, REB). Matthew reverses Luke's order (Luke 7.22) with regard to seeing and hearing. For Luke, seeing comes first. For Matthew, as we have observed, the Messiah of the word is primary to the Messiah of deed. There is also a connection between Jesus's ministry and that of those who are sent. The commission in 10.8 says, 'Heal the sick, raise the dead, cleanse lepers, drive out demons.' This sounds very much like Paul's final commission to the Philippians, 'All that you have heard me say or seen me do, put into practice' (Philippians 4.9). And the next section of the Gospel, the discourse to those who are sent, assumes that practice.

Verse 9.35 brings to an end the literary section that began at 4.23. It is linked to the discourse that follows, by a call to discipleship pictured as a call to labourers needed for a harvest. The harvest itself is identified as the people who are harassed and helpless, like sheep without a shepherd. France (1985) heads this section: 'The parallel ministry of the disciples.' Hill sees the emphasis being 'On Mission and Martyrdom' (Hill 1972, p. 184). Minear believes that 'perhaps this chapter should be called a manual for martyrs' (1984, p. 71). Hagner (1993) believes that the discourse begins with mission instructions, but soon turns to questions around persecution, name calling and the relationship between division and discipleship (pp. 267ff.). 'To engage in the mission of Jesus means also to follow him in the experience of hostility and rejection' (p. 262). From this we might expect that we shall continue to see the parallel description of Jesus's ministry and that of the Church, and that the section will be weighted in favour of the problems of ministry rather than its joys, in contrast to 9.15.

In terms of content, as opposed to the experience of the disciples, the key accent is identification with Jesus. The message to be proclaimed is the same as that proclaimed by both John and Jesus. The charge to them at 10.1 is reiterated at 10.8 and is clearly important. Notably it directs the disciples towards illness and infirmity. It does include an instruction to proclaim the presence of the Kingdom of Heaven, but there is no mention of belief, repentance or sin (cf. Mark 6.7–13). These disciples are agents of Jesus's compassion and pity (9.36). He is concerned with their suffering rather than their sin.

To do

If you have experience of a Christian community, is it more interested in sin than suffering? Do you think that is a legitimate question?

Matthew leaves his naming of the twelve disciples late, as opposed to the other evangelists. This is presumably to place the list of disciples next to their function and expectations. There is much discussion and perplexity about the instruction in 10.5–6 to restrict the mission to 'the lost sheep of the house of Israel' (cf. 15.24). This compares uneasily with the final instruction to the disciples at 28.19 to go to all nations. 'Lost sheep', with its echoes of Ezekiel 34.11–31, suggests the whole people rather than a specific group. Although only Matthew, in the Gospels, includes this restriction, there is an echo here also of Romans 1.16: to the Jew first and then the Gentile (cf. Romans 2.9, 3.1, 9.1–6), and from earlier in the Gospel (9.36). The most obvious explanation is reference to the two-track strategy of combining the mission of Jesus and the Church. Here we have the historic instructions of Jesus. Later we see the understanding that has developed in the Church of a mission to all peoples. There have been other concessions to Gentiles in the Gospel to date. The magi who come in chapter 2 as the first foreigners to visit Jesus are one example. The fact that most of Jesus's ministry is conducted in 'Galilee of the Gentiles', as it was known, is another. Also, we have the example of a healing miracle in a Gentile territory (8.28–34).

One way to read the actual discourse would be to see it as a set of answers to questions raised by the first Christian ministers. This is a new venture and Christian ministry is undeveloped and varies from community to community. The only ministers named as a class, apart from the apostles, the twelve, who are in any case a representative group both of Israel, and of the new ministry, are prophets, wise men and teachers, named together at 23.34 (cf. 10.41). Perhaps there is a group of Christian scribes, distinguishable from *their* scribes, if indeed that is the intended force of 7.29. In any case many questions must have been raised, since the 'ministry' of the Pharisees, which might have been the only model for many of Matthew's congregation, is so heavily criticized. Many see a distinction between vv 5–16, dealing with questions more appropriate to the immediate mission, and vv 16–42 dealing with more general questions about discipleship, apostleship and mission. A further division is possible at v 23.

To do

Read through Matthew 10.5–42. Make a list of the questions to which these 'instructions' might function as responses. So, for example, initial

> questions might include: where shall we go?
> What shall we say? Or, perhaps, is our message
> going to be exactly the same as yours? When you
> have completed your list, see if you can make
> another list of questions that might be raised
> by new ministers today. Are there any similari-
> ties? Do the answers given in Matthew's account
> satisfy any questions you think might be raised
> today?

Compared with Luke's version, Matthew appears
to have very little interest in the immediate mission
he claims to be speaking about. There is no description of what actually happened to the disciples and
no report back afterwards. 'At the conclusion of
the discourse it is *Jesus* who goes out teaching and
preaching (11.1)' (Hare 1993, p. 113). This leaves
the impression that Matthew is once again speaking theoretically and generally, and that we are not
reading about a specific occasion. Matthew 10.16–
25 describes situations of violent hostility to the
apostles. There is no such report in Mark; at least
not in the parallel account. What Matthew does
is import into his account material from Mark 13
(vv 9–13), which in Mark's Gospel is related to the
signs of the end of the age. Perhaps Matthew wants
to claim that the very proclamation of the Kingdom
is a sign of the end of the age in its own right, or
he wants to reinforce the point dramatically that
the message of Christianity is counter-cultural and

threatening, and uses readily available apocalyptic language to express that. He may also be wanting to create a literary context in which the immediate mission has cosmic significance. In any case there is a sense of the inevitability of opposition and suffering. Commentators generally ascribe this to the actual situation of Matthew's congregation and their experience of persecution at the hands of the Jewish authorities.

There are two consolations for persecuted apostles or missionaries. One is that the right words will be given them to defend themselves when accused and brought to court. The expression 'Spirit of your Father' is unique to Matthew. It would be wrong to make an easy comparison with Luke's use of Holy Spirit. For Luke, Holy Spirit is a key engine of growth, vitality and strategic direction in the Church and as such it appears throughout the Gospel and Acts some 53 times. Spirit appears in Mark's Gospel just four times and in Matthew five times, and clearly therefore does not occupy the same function as in Luke. On the other hand, the term Father, which occurs once in Mark and three times in Luke, occurs in Matthew 20 times. In 10.20 the phrase implies a close and caring relationship with God. This Gospel does emphasize the *providence* of the Father (6.26, 32–4; so Senior 1998, p. 118). Exodus 4.12 may give an Old Testament model. The second word of assurance is found in v 22: 'Whoever endures to the end will be saved.' The theme of endurance under suffering is a central one in apocalyptic writings.

The cross saying at 10.38 puzzles many commentators. It is not until 16.21 that Jesus announces his passion, and the mention of taking up a cross as a condition of discipleship at 16.24 makes sense in that context, though even then we must wait till 20.19 to see a clear description. Hagner is probably right in seeing v 39 as a kind of exegesis of v 38, since 'to take up one's cross is to follow in the footsteps of Jesus, who is the model of radical obedience and self-denial' (1993, p. 293). Perhaps we may go further and see here a third kind of consolation: namely, that in following a way of suffering we are, in fact, following Jesus's way closely. This was certainly a consolation for suffering Christians in other places (cf. 1 Peter 2.23–4).

To do

See if you can find any first-hand testimony from Christians who have suffered persecution for their faith in modern times. What sustained them? Do you see links between Matthew's situation and theirs?

We are introduced in the final verse of the chapter to another of Matthew's favourite designations, 'little ones'. The concept occurs several times and in several forms (11.25; 18.6, 10, 14; 19.13–14; 25.40, 45). Here it refers to the disciples, but in other places, as we shall see, it refers to those for whom God has most concern. Love of the least is to become a criterion of discipleship.

How, then, should we summarize this section of the Gospel? Jesus calls disciples because of his compassion towards the shepherdless crowds, and in the first instance the lost sheep of Israel. They are to extend his own work of teaching, preaching and healing. They have his authority and commission but might expect also to suffer the same rejection and suffering that he did. To be worthy of him they must intentionally take up a cross and lose their lives for his sake. They must travel light and, as travellers, be vulnerable. 'They serve as shepherds (9.36), harvesters (9.38), healers, preachers, exorcists, beggars, sheep, servants, criminals, refugees, prophets, slaves. What a galaxy of epithets! What a range of tasks!' (Minear 1984, p. 72).

To do

Think back to why Nikki is here, and what sense she may have made of this part of the Gospel. How does being a follower, as Jesus describes it in Matthew's account, differ from that she held? You may like to think about the categories of 'cost' and 'suffering'. If you were arranging a series of talks on being baptized as an adult today, to a group of people that included Nikki, how might you use this section of the Gospel?

4

Jesus and Disappointment

Before he was ordained as a Christian minister, David had had a reasonably secure and successful career as a loss adjuster. He has always been a churchgoer and when an increasing sense of frustration with the predictability and bureaucracy of his work coincided with a vocations weekend at his local church, he decided to go along. He was inspired by what he experienced, felt that he had a call to a Christian ministry that was described in exciting terms, and after a lengthy selection process and training schedule he found himself in charge of a local church for the first time. The church in question was a little run down and poorly attended, but David decided he was going to change all that. Fired by his recent experience of God's call, and Bible study that focused on the contemporary relevance of terms like 'The Kingdom of God' in the political and social sphere, he set about building up his church. However, things did not go as he expected. There was no revival. The people who already came did not want to be disturbed by lots of new ideas and those who did not come seemed quite happy to keep it that way. After a year or so, in conversation with his spiritual director, David confessed his huge disappointment, verging on depression. He was told to read Matthew's Gospel, and especially the portions leading up to chapter 13. Disappointment is no new thing. With this perspective, David began to read the passages recommended.

Read Matthew 11 and 12

At the end of Luke's account of the missionary venture the 72 who were sent out 'came back jubilant' (Luke 10.17). It had all been a great success. The dire warnings of the previous verses about rejection had proved to be without foundation. It was such a success that Jesus himself was moved to 'exult in the Holy Spirit' and give thanks to God, 'the Lord of Heaven and earth' (10.21). Luke, the eternal optimist, is telling a story of continuing growth and success that will continue through the book of Acts. There are questions about how far this matches reality, but it is clear that Matthew's view of reality is quite different.

After the apostles have been sent on their mission there is no joyous return. There is an ominous silence, suggesting that some or all the prophecies of rejection have come to pass. That feeling is confirmed as we read through the next few chapters. John the Baptist's disciples question whether Jesus really is the Messiah (11.3) and that gives opportunity to set the Christian mission in a wider context of the rejection of the prophets, leading to the imprisonment of John himself. This is followed by a series of denunciations for various towns where the message has been proclaimed but there has been no positive response (11.20–4). Chapter 12 begins with argument and controversy about the interpretation of the Sabbath law. In the Lukan equivalent (Luke 6.11) this provokes the scribes and Pharisees to discuss with one another 'what they could do to Jesus'. Matthew's conclusion is far darker and, more in line with Mark, they plotted to bring about Jesus's death (Matthew 12.14). There follows a series of sayings about division. Jesus is accused of being an agent of Beelzebub (12.24). The section ends with the defiant cry of Jesus: 'He who is not with me is against me, and he who does not gather with me scatters' (12.30). This is the exact opposite of the Markan saying, 'He who is not against us is on our side' (Mark 9.40), and presents a much more heightened demand.

Throughout these chapters there is no direct response from the crowds. Only the Pharisees respond, although Jesus is in the public sphere, either in the synagogue or elsewhere, and he does address crowds (12.46). The disciples continue to have a special place. Jesus even disavows his family in their favour (12.49). This is in distinction to

Mark who presents the disciples as uncomprehending. The disciples in Matthew are those Jesus trusts to take the message forward. His rejection foreshadows theirs. We have the sense that Matthew's Church feels very much under threat.

To do

If, as many scholars think, the 'atmosphere' of Matthew gives us insight into the context for which it was written, what context if any do you think might match that atmosphere today? Might it be churches that are facing persecution today, or churches whose message is not appealing to their societies, for example?

There is a wider question here which is relevant beyond the narrow confines of first-century Syria, and that is the frustration that many Christians feel when a message that has struck them so forcibly, prompted changes in their outlook and world view that could even be described as a transformation, fails to have any impact at all on their fellows. In Matthew's situation it is not a complete disaster. The more subtle message is that those who might have been expected to be attracted are not, and some of those often disregarded by the religious establishment are the ones attracted. So, the unrepentant cities and the 'wise and learned' do not understand the message (11.20–1), but it is understood by the simple and lowly (11.25). This should not be taken to mean that the wise and learned do not feature at all in the early Christian congregations. This is not a sociological point. Matthew himself is obviously an example of someone who is learned. The point is that no one can claim privilege as a result of anything other than faith that shows fruits.

By the end of chapter 12 a number of questions have been raised that would be easily recognizable to David. We might summarize some of them as follows.

- Why is it that some respond, and others do not?
- Should the Church consist only of those who have made the most definite commitment to be 'with us'?
- Given that the probable main target audience was the Jewish religious community, how should the Church respond to rejection, especially from this quarter?
- If the Kingdom has really come, how can we explain the ongoing presence of evil as represented in the rejection, and if the results are so modest?
- What is the role of divine judgement in this situation, and what if anything is God doing about this?

Chapter 13 contains the third of the five discourses identified by scholars. It is sometimes described as containing the 'parables of the kingdom'. What it amounts to is a commentary, by Jesus the Interpreter, on the kinds of question raised above in a new idiom. This is the first time in the Gospel that we hear of Jesus speaking in parables.

Parables proved to be a rich focus of scholarly interest in the twentieth century. The study could be regarded as a side effect of form criticism. Form critics were interested in how the different kinds of materials that form our finished Gospels were preserved before being written down. Given that a period of at least 30 years transpired between the events of Jesus's life and the Gospel accounts of them, this is an important historical study. Initially the stories about Jesus would have been passed on orally, but in what context did that happen? Was it that some stories were told in particular places he had visited and were in some sense deposited there? Were the stories preserved in preaching or worship contexts? Did some kinds of story form collections before being written down? Form critics approach their task by first identifying different kinds or genres of material. They then suggest situations in real life where that kind of material might have been preserved, and on the basis of that they reach conclusions about how historically accurate it might be (knowing that in some story-telling contexts additions and alterations are more likely than in others). We have already seen the suggestion, for example, that miracle stories tend to get 'more miraculous' as stories are passed on. This kind of study helps us to appreciate the incredible skill of the Gospel writers who brought these sources together into a readable narrative that was both persuasive and attractive, though by the time they wrote, scholars believe that there had already been some 'editorial' work resulting in four main sources.

One of the genres identified by form critics was parables. There are generally thought to be four sources for the first three (Synoptic) Gospels. These are the Gospel of Mark; material common to Matthew and Luke not present in Mark (called Q by scholars); material found only in Luke (L), and material found only in Matthew's Gospel (M). Parables are found in all of these sources, and that is one reason for considering them to be authentic. There are questions, though, about how the Church might have altered, or added to, Jesus's originals.

Until the nineteenth century, parables had been thought of as straightforward allegories. So, for example, St Augustine, commenting on the parable of the Good Samaritan, saw the traveller as being Adam, Jerusalem the heavenly city and the robbers as the devil. The Samaritan was Jesus and the Levite represented the Old Testament priesthood. The modern critical approach does not believe this is how the parables are meant to be read. Julicher believed that any suggestion of allegory is the result of later church additions. Originally parables had just one point. They were extended similes, not extended allegories.

Dodd and Jeremias saw that single point as being connected to the concept of the Kingdom of God/

Heaven, which is how many of them begin ('The Kingdom of God may be compared . . .'). Dodd believed that what they demonstrated was that the Kingdom had been realized in their midst as a present reality, and that their purpose was to face people with a challenge as to how they would respond to that. His classic definition of a parable is a model of clarity. 'At its simplest the parable is a metaphor or simile drawn from nature or common life, arresting the hearer by its vividness or strangeness, and leaving the mind in sufficient doubt about its precise application to tease it into active thought' (Dodd 1961, p. 16).

Dodd's 'realized eschatology': his understanding that the Kingdom had been inaugurated in the ministry of Jesus, was a radical idea in its time and challenged the view that the Kingdom's coming was a totally future event. Many scholars have been reluctant to abandon the future expectation element of the Kingdom, and that has influenced the view of some as to the meaning of the parables in Matthew 13. Hill would be typical in his interpretation of the parable of the sower. 'The accent of the parable is not on how people should hear the word of God, but on the fact that the Kingdom of God will certainly come, with a harvest beyond all expectation, but by way of failure, disappointment and loss' (Hill 1972, p. 225). This is in the context of 'explaining why the Kingdom, inaugurated by Jesus, has not yet arrived in glory, and why, in particular, its results in Jesus's ministry are at this point without grandeur and power' (Hill, pp. 223–4). In other words, the parables in chapter 13 are a way of countering disappointment.

There is a tendency in this and similar accounts to misunderstand the significance of *parousia* and to confuse *parousia* and *Kingdom*. *Parousia* is a Greek word meaning 'presence' or 'being at hand' but is often translated in English as 'second coming'. There are many claims for its being a technical term with a specific theological meaning and we shall return to that discussion later. A strong case can be made, however, for saying that the signs of the Kingdom's presence are really what Matthew is demonstrating in the way he describes the ministry of Jesus, and that the present reality of the Kingdom is emphasized by his insistence that Jesus is the Messiah: the one whom the tradition asserts will bring in the Kingdom. Matthew's additions to the Passion Narrative are a way, we shall see, of claiming that the Resurrection, rather than whatever the *parousia* might mean, is the key sign of the Kingdom's having begun. To that extent, at this point in the story, judgement is still a future expectation, and that is certainly a theme of the later parables.

Debates about eschatology characterized much New Testament scholarly discussion in the middle of the last century and few would claim that its questions have been satisfactorily answered or that such answers as exist are universally accepted. The context for the debate was an approach to Bible criticism, in use since the nineteenth century, that made primary use of the critical tools used by historians. Their main question was: what would this have meant to the people who first heard or read it? Hence there was special interest, in this approach, in contemporary expectations of a return of Jesus.

This seemed to David to be something of a distraction. He had never, if he were honest, lived in the expectation of an early return of Jesus. He confided as much to his wife Jo. He chose to do so as she returned from her monthly afternoon at the Reading Circle, a book club that David rather dismissed as a cover for a wine-tasting afternoon, but on this occasion Jo had advice for him that he took seriously. She said, if this Gospel of Matthew were one of our book group books, the kind of questions we would be asking about it are quite different. We would want to ask about the characterization, the way the plot develops, the way the author persuades us to his point of view. In fact, this is one direction that Gospel criticism has been taking.

Current interest in literary approaches to the Gospels, together with the invitation of Matthew 13 itself, 'Why do you speak to them in parables?' (13.10), prompts us to look at not just the *form* of the parables but rather their *function* in the rhetoric of the Gospel, and that leads to new ways of articulating its Christology. Senior describes Jesus in this part of the Gospel as 'Jesus the Revealer' (1998, p. 131). That is what he sees Jesus doing. But does Jesus use them in order to reveal truths about the mystery of the Kingdom, or does he use them as if they were riddles or crossword clues, to make them less accessible to people who do not have the requisite skill to unlock them? Matthew 13.10–17 gives us clues. Here Matthew has changed and expanded Mark's version (Mark 4.11–12). The significant change is the replacing of the Greek *ina* (so that) with *oti* (because). These two small Greek words signify quite different approaches. In Mark's version Jesus speaks in parables to veil their meaning – *so that* they may not understand. In Matthew's version, he speaks in parables *because* they do not understand.

In modern terms, we might describe this difference in terms of nature or nurture. Mark believes that the 'they' referred to in his Gospel are hardwired to resist the Gospel. They have an in-built propensity to resist it. It is part of their very nature. Philosophers call this approach 'determinism'. In religious terminology, scholars of the Reformation would have referred to this as 'predestination'. Matthew, on the other hand, believes that his 'they' have been taught to resist the Gospel of the Kingdom by cultural and religious leaders who have misled them. At the level of seeing, hearing and doing, they have come to accept that religion demands that sacrifice is more important than mercy; that reciting the right liturgy is guarantee of being on God's side, and that religious rules outweigh the common humanity of feeding hungry people if they happen to be hungry on the wrong day. And so the parables are an attempt to puncture this at the level of *understanding* – a key term in this Gospel. And the strategy for that is to present profound truths in a way that will appeal first to experience and emotion and through that to intellect. Seen in this light, the parables, generally, are a continuation of the struggle against the Jewish religious leaders, and any other 'old' ideas of religion imported with Gentile converts. They are capable of interpretation at a number of levels. There is also an intentional division in chapter 13 between vv 34 and 36. Until v 34 Jesus is addressing the crowds. After v 36 he has withdrawn to a house with his disciples. Unlike Mark's portrayal, Matthew shows Jesus trusting the disciples with the message and assuring himself that they have *understood*. That key term is used repeatedly (vv 13, 14, 19, 23, and in summary, 51).

To do

How important do you think it is to distinguish between nature and nurture when it comes to moral issues? Are some people born to be evil, for example? The tabloid press might have us believe that sometimes. Can you think of examples? Are there people who are 'beyond redemption'? On the other hand, are there people whose characters seem to have goodness imprinted in their DNA? What are the implications of this for religion, and particularly for Christian ministry?

A literary approach to the Gospel would also want to explore the connection between this discourse and the material that precedes it. The bullet points on p. 71 provided a summary of some of the questions raised in the preceding chapters and we can see how the parables are used to respond to those questions.

Read Matthew 13.3–9, 18–23

This is one of the best known of all the parables. Matthew actually calls it the parable of the sower (13.18). His source is Mark 4.1–9, 13–20. That appears also to have been Luke's source (Luke 8.4–8, 11–15). In a sense it is a strange title because it draws attention to the aspect of the story that does not have an equivalent in the explanation. A modern reader, having heard the story without the explanation, may conclude that the problems lie in the indiscriminate actions of the sower, who broadcasts the seed all over the place rather than focusing it on the areas where it is most likely to grow, and certainly that is how David might read it, but that is not necessarily where Matthew wants us to look. The point of the parable is to highlight the difficulties any sower has when sowing the word, thus continuing the theme of the previous chapters in a different idiom.

We see described three different kinds of soil which yield different results. In addition, we see that some seed does not even make it to the soil but settles on the path for a while before it disappears completely; and that even in the good soil there is a varied response, differing between a 30 per cent and a 100 per cent yield. Interestingly Matthew reverses Mark's way of describing the yield in the good soil. For Mark the yield builds up to a great crescendo (Mark 4.8). For Matthew there appears to be a different mood. Perhaps we could read into this: although there is, in some places, a 100 per cent yield, actually, in others, there is also a 60 per cent and a 30 per cent, but they still represent a harvest. Take a reality check. It is of course the explanation which is of most interest. Form and redaction critics told us, as a rule, that this 'explanation' was a late addition; a Church creation excusing the Church for its lack of progress, perhaps quoting an early sermon. More recently there has been caution about accepting that parables only have one point, and should not be regarded as allegories. This parable cries out for such an interpretation, and when it appears, it does not seem unnatural or forced. France sees no reason why Jesus might not have been responsible for it (France 1985; see also Hagner 1993, pp. 364–5).

Matthew tells us that the word being sown is the word of the Kingdom. Those last three words he has added to Mark. He then adds something else which is typical of him. The seed that falls on the path is not just carried away from people by Satan's agency, as Mark says, but rather it never hits the soil because the people have failed to understand. They are incapable of receiving it. The Greek word means 'to gain an insight into'. This is the capacity they do not have.

The rocky ground is the place of superficiality. The interesting thing here is that for a while this must have seemed to be the most successful seed of all. It quickly sprang up. But equally quickly it dies off. Matthew and Mark use different words from Luke to describe the trouble that comes upon those who have insufficient root. Mark and Matthew use the Greek words *diogmos* and *thlipsis*. Luke uses the Greek word *peirasmos*. The first two terms are widely distributed in the apocalyptic tradition and can be used to describe the kind of anguish that will precede the end of the age. They are the most serious terms that the New Testament employs to describe persecution. The word that Luke uses has a different sense of trial. It is a word used in the temptation accounts (Matthew 4.1, Luke 4.2) to describe what Jesus is going through in the wilderness. There is some debate about whether this word can be used to describe actual persecution or harassment. Much of this is related to its use in 1 Peter where *peirasmos* describes the sufferings described there (1 Peter 1.6). On such evidence as this, scholars try to imagine the context of Matthew's Church.

The next kind of sowing is what we might nowadays understand as the prosperity gospel. People opt for the Gospel because they misunderstand what the Kingdom is about and are loathe to leave behind the attractions of the Kingdom of earth: glamour and wealth, even though they run the risk of increasing anxiety. This is effectively a re-run of the teaching in chapter 7, in a different idiom. The good soil still does not produce what you might expect. In some cases there is still only a 30 per cent crop. This is describing a reality which is perplexing, and again perhaps points to other aspects of Matthew's Church. It is a mixed community in its commitment and enthusiasm, and perhaps even in what Matthew would call its understanding. The next parable goes on to suggest that it is mixed in other ways as well.

At this point it is worth mentioning one interesting theory about how the structure of the chapter progresses. B. Gerhardsson (*New Testament Studies*, 19, 1972–3, pp. 16–37) proposes that the six parables following the opening parable of the sower should be read as expansions of aspects of that parable. So the parable of the wheat and the tares picks up the seed on the path theme, the mustard seed and the leaven in the lump parables relate to the rocky ground; the treasure and the pearl relate to the seed among thorns, and the dragnet the good seed.

To do

Read through the rest of the chapter. How convinced are you by Gerhardsson's idea? There certainly appear to be some connecting themes even if the absolute correspondence is patchy. Then think about any religious congregation that you know. How would you match its 'understanding' to the categories outlined in the sower parable?

The next parable, the wheat and the weeds (13.24–30, 37–43), is peculiar to Matthew, and certainly focuses on the theme of judgement. It is notable that this parable refers not to the Church, or the disciples or even 'this generation'. Like the most memorable of the judgement parables it describes the judgement of the world (13.38; cf. 25.32). As already noted, this is in the future at this point in the story. Whether Matthew intends (as does John) that the Resurrection be seen as the last judgement (John 12.32), rather than some future event beyond that, is not made clear. The two accounts are also similar in that for Matthew judgement invariably involves division. In the case of the wheat and the weeds, there may have been a presenting issue in terms of questions about purity and church membership, but this is a chance to relate the question, if that is what is being asked, to a wider perspective. If the parable were to be told nowadays it might relate to issues around the conditions that churches should impose on church membership. Can anyone join or should there be tests of faith to maintain purity of doctrine and intention? Is the church a congregation of the righteous or a *corpus mixtum*? However, it would be wrong to read this as Matthew's intention. We have no preceding evidence to suggest division in the church itself, or that lots of people are joining without proper credentials.

The notable features of this parable are the uses it makes of the apocalyptic tradition. The phrase which is translated in some Bibles as the 'end of time' (REB) or 'the end of the world' (NJB) is more correctly translated (as NIV), the 'end of the age', or the 'close of the age'. This is important to readers in English, since it does not predict the end of all existence, but rather the end of this age and the beginning of another. The content of the new age is what has been described as the Kingdom of Heaven. Harvest is a traditional image of judgement at this foreseen time (Joel 3.13, Jeremiah 51.33, Hosea 6.11, 2 Esdras 4.28–9). Jesus has the apocalyptic title Son of Man, and here is described as the sower. Judgement invariably accompanies the transition between ages, since one of the reasons for longing for a new age is that natural justice is seen to be lacking in the present age. Bad things happen to good people and bad people often seem to thrive. The judgement at the end of the age is one way of coping with that. Each will get their just deserts. Notably, there is no equivalent explanation of the discussion between the farmers' men and their master, but if there had been such an explanation it might have been along these lines.

To do

Put yourself in David's shoes. At this point in the chapter what do you think he will have been encouraged by? What might cause him to revise his early optimism about Church growth? What new insights might he have gained? Do you know people who are depressed about the state of the Church or the world? How could this chapter help them to cope do you think? You might like to consider how it encourages a broad perspective, a bigger picture; how it offers an inspiring message; how it describes God in such positive and pro-active terms, and the encouragement it offers not to dismiss small initiatives and small steps forward.

Two other short parables in the collection are found elsewhere in the Synoptic Gospels (the mustard seed, Mark 4.30–2, Luke 13.18–19; the leaven in Luke 13.20–1). The mustard seed appeared in a rabbinic proverb to denote the tiniest thing. The message here seems to be that even the tiniest beginnings can have great potential. The leaven has a similar encouragement. Even when it looks as though nothing is happening, the yeast is working within the dough. Leaven is used again at 16.6 to warn against the insidious evil of the Sadducees and Pharisees, but its use here is more positive.

Apocalyptic writing developed to maintain hope for people whose experience was at odds with their faith, and to encourage them not to give up but to maintain all that faith demanded of them. The drift towards apocalyptic in this chapter is consistent with that. The concept of a Kingdom of Heaven is related through Old Testament tradition to the United Kingdom of David, seen in retrospect as a golden age, with which the present compares badly. In the Kingdom there will be a rigorous return to Covenant principles of justice and mercy. There will be an end to suffering, and perhaps most importantly of all, to those who are questioning even the existence of God or who are so disillusioned that they question the point of religion; in the inauguration of the Kingdom there is definite evidence of God's concern and action.

The remaining parables of the chapter, the treasure, the pearl and the net, are peculiar to Matthew and interesting on that account. They continue the theme of encouragement – after all, this is written to people who do not consider themselves to be among the condemned but rather among the vindicated. Both describe the special joy of being a disciple. The first is an accidental find. The second is a more professional discovery by someone who is a pearl trader. This may refer to the different routes church members have taken to reach discipleship. Both 'give up' something in order to have that which is of greater value. That could be an allusion to the disciples who have 'given up' things in order to follow Jesus, which has greater worth. The dragnet repeats the point of the parable of the wheat and the weeds in a different setting but with common phrases. Some scholars see the reference to the householder as a parable, in which case it might conclude the collection in parallel with the opening parable of the sower (so France 1985, p. 234).

To do

Looking back over this collection of parables, look at them as Jo's book group might. What do you think they have told us about Jesus? You might think about what they have told us about his method as a teacher, and about the importance of *understanding*. You might think we have learned more about his priorities, in which case you may want to spell them out. You may think that the Church is the main focus rather than Jesus, in which case what is Jesus saying to it that counts as a development from what has gone before? Or you may think that as the account begins with the world and describes the world in the judgement parables, that the world is the main focus of concern, in which case what is Jesus asking the Church to say to it?

5

Jesus and Peter

Rowena has been watching a televised dramatization of the growth of the early Christian Church. She has found it both interesting and inspirational. Her parents were devout Roman Catholics and she was brought up and confirmed in that church, though nowadays her attendance is sporadic at best. However, she cannot resist the opportunity the television series affords to check her response to Christianity at this point in her life. One of the things that has fascinated and even surprised her is the leading part that (in the TV series at least) Peter plays in the whole thing. This has rekindled ancient memories of church, and it has prompted a desire to know more about the place of Peter in the Gospels. A few enquiries have revealed that it is Matthew's Gospel that has most to say about Peter, and so Rowena has decided that she wants to know more about what she once took for granted and has more recently become suspicious of.

Of course, disciples feature in all four Gospels and Peter is always the first on the list. Only in John's Gospel is he not also the first to be called. In that Gospel, the first disciples are originally disciples of John, one of whom turns out to be Peter's brother Andrew. It is he who brings Peter to Jesus who immediately nicknames him the Rock (John 1.40–2). In the early days of Jesus's ministry there appear to have been many disciples (Luke 6.17), but some fell away disillusioned (John 6.60–1, 66). These are distinguished from 'the twelve', of whom Peter's leadership is clear, and accompanied sometimes by fierce loyalty. That is evidenced in all the Gospels (John 6.68, Mark 8.32). As ministry develops in Matthew and Mark, at least, 'the twelve' are identified as 'the disciples' (Wilkins 1992, p. 177). The importance of there being twelve is a clear reference to the twelve tribes of Israel, in the tradition, and a way of claiming that a new Israel-like community is being formed. Peter's name is mentioned in the New Testament 210 times and he is by far the most frequently named individual disciple (compare Paul who is mentioned just 162 times). It is Peter who gives the next few chapters of Matthew its distinctive character.

In truth, scholars find some difficulty in determining a theme for those next few chapters of Matthew's Gospel, from the end of the parables discourse in chapter 13 to the beginning of the next discourse in chapter 18. Matthew follows Mark's order in Mark chapters 6–9 through this section and that has the effect of disturbing a carefully thought-through presentation up to this point, because Mark's strategy is different from Matthew's. The most obvious difference is in the way each author has led readers to view the disciples.

Mark presents them as uncomprehending. They have been privileged to receive the Kingdom secrets but do not understand what they are hearing (Mark 4.13, 7.17–18). Luke has a much wider definition of discipleship. Luke 6.13 describes how Jesus chose the twelve from among a bigger crowd of disciples. This bigger group is referred to again throughout the Gospel (e.g. 19.37–9) and 'disciple' is effectively a synonym for 'believer' in Acts. Whereas Jesus sends out the twelve on the first missionary project in Matthew and Mark, Luke has him send out 72 others (Luke 10.1–16). Matthew portrays Jesus as the teacher of the disciples, and each of the teaching discourses is directed towards them. For Matthew they are the understanding recipients of Kingdom secrets (13.52, 16.12, 17.13). This means that he has to adapt his narrative to incorporate a tough love approach, of supporting them while chiding them for their 'little faith' (a favourite term for Matthew, e.g. 6.30, 8.26, 16.8, 17.20). If applied to Matthew's church, this could be said to describe a practical assessment of church leadership. It has been commissioned, but has all the traits of human imperfection. In other words, it is both realistic and pastoral. Peter is very definitely the spokesman for the twelve, and the most noticeable specially Matthean elements in chapters 14–18 concern Peter.

Read Matthew 14.1–32

This section, more diffuse, less focused and more difficult to describe as a whole than those we have seen so far, begins with an account of the death of John the Baptist. That may be significant in itself as part of the structure of the Gospel, in that this section is 'bracketed' by the death of John and the crucifixion of Jesus (Case-Winters 2015, p. 188). The death of John is clearly significant and can be seen either as the end or the beginning of an era. We then move to the first of two feeding miracles (14.13–21). The second is later in the same section (15.32–9) and the two are clearly to be seen in sequence and with joint significance (16.9–11). The feeding of the five thousand is a miracle that is recounted in all four Gospels and is clearly very important in the tradition, perhaps because of its eucharistic symbolism. It has many layers of symbolic allusion. It refers back to the Exodus tradition – the feeding takes place in a desert or wilderness (*eremos* in Greek, the word from which we get the English word hermit) – with its provision of manna as food for the hungry escapees. It may also point to the traditions around a messianic banquet (e.g. Isaiah 25.6–9). In some Jewish messianic feast traditions there is mention of bread and fish in the messianic feast. The verbs 'took', 'blessed', 'broke', 'gave' are the central verbs of eucharistic liturgy, and the word *klasmata* for fragments is the word used to refer to the eucharistic elements in the *Didache* (Did. 9.3–4). In the historical narrative this is a re-emphasis of Jesus's credentials as the first act of a post-John the Baptist era, and is a reaffirmation of the answer to John's disciples' question: are you he who is to come or shall we look for another (9.3)? In the Church narrative, it may speak of the priority of 'feeding' in Church ministry, and perhaps even the root of that feeding in the Eucharist. Notably it is the disciples who distribute the bread that Jesus has blessed and broken.

To do

If you belong to a church tradition, how important is the Eucharist, Holy Communion or the Mass within that tradition? Given Matthew's emphasis on teaching, how does that fit with the tradition you have received? If you were starting a new Christian Church denomination what place would the Eucharist have in it?

Rowena has discovered that her interest in Peter, and his link with the churches we know, has led to wider exploration about discipleship and the way in which church was experienced in the forming Church.

Following the first feeding miracle we have one of the accounts that centres on Peter. In this passage

Peter attempts to walk on the water. This is preceded by Jesus's going up the mountain to pray alone. Some commentators want to make much of this and relate it to other mountain settings (e.g. Senior 1998, p. 170), but Matthew is simply following Mark here. The fact that he goes to pray by himself may be more interesting, since in this Gospel he only does that in relation to his imminent suffering and death elsewhere (26.36, 39, 42, 44). The story shared between Matthew and Mark is that the disciples are out at sea on the boat, struggling against a head wind. Jesus sees them from his mountain and walks across the water to them. After failing to recognize him originally, they eventually do so after he has declared '*ego eimi*' ('it is I'). Then Matthew departs from Mark. In Mark, Jesus gets into the boat and calm is restored. The incident demonstrates the disciples' lack of understanding and closed minds. Matthew, by contrast, inserts a section in which Peter asks: 'Lord, if it is you, tell me to come to you over the water' (14.28). Jesus beckons him and Peter attempts to do what Jesus had done. However, he is overcome by fear and begins to sink. He calls out '*Kyrie, soson me*', 'Lord, save me'. Jesus catches hold of him and they both get into the boat. Jesus rebukes him for his lack of faith, but the disciples, far from misunderstanding, understand perfectly and say: 'you must be the Son of God!' (14.33).

At one level this is reminiscent of the stilling of the storm miracle previously recounted (8.23–7).

However, although here there is a head wind, the boat is not perceived as being in danger of sinking. The danger arises because of Peter's audacious request, and his failure to complete. The cry has the same liturgical ring, and there is the same rebuke of little faith. This could be taken as another example of Jesus demonstrating his power. The fearful image of the sea and the fact that this happens at the darkest time of night underline that (cf. Psalm 107.25–31). But alongside that is surely a message about Jesus 'seeing' the plight of the early Church and coming to accompany it (rather than rescue – at this stage there is nothing to be rescued from). Peter's conversation suggests that Jesus is beckoning the Church on, in the midst of heavy weather, to take new initiatives in faith, and the leadership is right to want to do that and ready enough to set out on new courses. However, fear overtakes faith and the project is in danger of stalling. But it does not, for at the last minute (this is the fourth watch of the night) Jesus intervenes. Notable is the pastoral word: 'do not be afraid' (14.27). This, the overwhelming message to combat lack of faith, is the fourth occurrence of seven such assurances in Matthew's Gospel (1.20, 8.26, 10.31, 14.27, 17.7, 28.5, 28.10), continuing what might be described as the overwhelming pastoral gospel message of the Old Testament (Jeremiah 30.10, Isaiah 43.1–4 and *passim*). Here it is combined with *ego eimi*, a reflection of the Old Testament name of God, and a further assurance in the face of little faith.

It has been suggested that Peter as the archetypal disciple here represents the situation of congregational members in Matthew's Church, and perhaps reflects more contemporary experience. Rowena had thought that her interest in Peter would centre on him receiving the keys of the Kingdom, but she has become fascinated by the picture of Peter (the Church?) walking on water (eggshells?).

To do

What message for disciples in the early or indeed the contemporary Church do you think this passage reveals? What word is used in v 31 to translate the Greek *distazo* in the version you are using? Some translate 'doubt', while others translate 'hesitate'. Both are possible. What difference do you think it makes to the interpretation of the passage and its relation to experience of discipleship today?

Now read Matthew 15.

This chapter begins with a passage critical of the Pharisees and scribes, in which Jesus is called to answer to them for the behaviour of his disciples, which, it is claimed, break ancient tradition by not adhering to a rule to wash their hands before eating. The triviality of the 'offence' gives opportunity to foreshadow his criticism of the Pharisees in chapter 23. It is Peter who acts as spokesman for the group when he asks for an explanation about an illustration that Jesus has used. This passage neither leads from what precedes it or properly introduces what follows.

Now we find Jesus 'abroad' in the region of Tyre and Sidon (modern Lebanon). The fact that Jesus is among foreigners is emphasized by his healing of a woman who is a foreigner. In itself, the incident with the foreign woman is a difficult one to read. Matthew alone calls her a Canaanite. This is rather like calling a present-day Scandinavian a Viking. The only possible reason would be to draw attention to her foreign-ness by recalling that the Canaanites were driven out of the land of promise by the Israelites. This harsh beginning is continued first by Jesus ignoring the woman's pleas for him to heal her daughter, despite her calling him Son of David, the ultimate Jewish title. Then he verbally refuses her. Finally, he is impressed sufficiently by her faith to do as she asks, and her daughter is healed. All of this seems out of keeping with the character of the compassionate Jesus, though it accords with the instructions to the disciples to restrict their initial mission to Israel (10.5–6).

Explanations include the following:

- This demonstrates that in the end faith and not ethnicity is what counts (Hagner 1993).
- This shows that persistence pays off but, actually, Jesus's response may not have been as

harsh as we take it to be. His response about giving food to the dogs may have been a popular saying like, 'charity begins at home', which Jesus wanted to test her with (Hare 1993).

- This should be read as a contrast to the religious leaders, described in the preceding passage as hypocrites (Senior 1998).

- Verse 24 is an aside to the disciples rather than a response to the woman, and 'written words cannot convey a twinkle in the eye, and it may be that Jesus was almost jocularly presenting her with the sort of language she might expect from a Jew to see how she would react' (France 1985, p. 250).

- This is an occasion when Jesus actually learns something himself and 'gained a wider vision of his calling' (Case-Winters 2015, p. 203).

To do

Note Jesus's compassionate acts and 'feeding' immediately following this incident. We understand that many members of Matthew's congregation were in fact Gentile. Put yourself in the place of one of them. Do any of these explanations convince you? Do you agree with Krister Stendhal (quoted by Hare, p. 179) that Christians are merely 'honorary Jews'? Bear in mind that, historically, the mission to the Gentiles was probably secondary.

The second of the feeding miracles follows on from this. There is a brief description of his healing ministry there (15.29–31) which concludes with the foreigners giving praise in their amazement to 'The God of Israel' (15.31). That context and the new numbers of people (4,000 men) and baskets (seven) has led to suggestions that the two miracles might represent the initial Jewish mission on the one hand, and the Gentile mission on the other. Peter only features briefly in chapter 15, but he has a major part in the following chapter.

In the declaration at Caesarea Philippi (Matthew 16.16; cf. Mark 8.29, Luke 9.20) Matthew has added to Peter's declaration that Jesus is the Messiah the words '[you are] the Son of the living God'. There is no parallel to 16.18–19 in which Jesus tells Peter that he is the rock on which his church will be built (the nearest comparison is John's account of his initial introduction to Jesus; John 1.42). Matthew shares with Mark and Luke the Transfiguration account in which Peter has a leading role. The discourse in chapter 18 has something to say about church discipline in a way that links 16.19 with 18.18. We could therefore say that one theme of interest in this section is the contribution that Peter makes to the story of Jesus in this Gospel. In so far as Peter is a representative of the disciples as a group (which is how Rowena has come to see him), this makes this section quite intentionally a story about discipleship. In this section the audiences are markedly different. The disciples are present on 18 occasions; the crowds are present only six times and the Pharisees only five times. Again, if we take the view that the story of the very early Church is being superimposed upon the story of the earthly Jesus, then the disciples here stand for the leaders in the Church, and it could perhaps be said that here Jesus is teaching the disciples how to be leaders in that Church.

Read Matthew 16.13–28

The 'incident at Caesarea Philippi' is crucial in each of the Synoptic Gospels. It marks the point at which the evidence which Jesus's ministry has provided as to who he is, and which has been described hitherto, has become overwhelming. Beyond this point the whole story moves towards its culmination in the Passion and Resurrection narratives. At this point there is an open declaration of Jesus's messiahship. This is the place that everything Matthew has written since 1.1 and 1.17–18 has been leading towards.

The area itself may or may not be significant. France tells us it was the centre of worship for the pagan god Pan (France 1985, p. 256) and that may give force to the title 'living' God, which is a Matthean addition to Mark. It is at the north-eastern point of Galilee, and therefore not far from where Matthew's community is probably situated. It is just about the furthest point in Galilee from Jerusalem, to which a journey now begins. But it may be simply historical fact. The section begins with an awkwardly phrased question: 'Who do people say that the Son of Man is?' This suggests that the meaning of 'Son of Man' is not self-evident. Various answers are given. Matthew alone includes Jeremiah among the possibilities. Jeremiah represents both loneliness and suffering sacrifice in the Old Testament. Theodore Robinson's classic description of him concludes 'for the full realization of Jeremiah's message, the world had to wait till that night when Jesus having supped, took the cup also saying, "This cup is the New Covenant in my blood." There is no fulfilment of the highest truth the Prophets had to offer apart from the Cross' (Robinson 1923/1967, p. 142). This sits well with what follows in Matthew.

It is Simon Peter who declares that Jesus is the Messiah, the Son of the living God. Matthew then adds his own material. Peter is to be the rock on which Jesus's *ekklesia* is to be built. The word play around the Greek word for rock is best understood as a nickname in the first instance. Peter is called Rocky. It could also be seen as his discipleship name as opposed to his given name. There has been great scholarly interest in the passage because of the part it plays in Roman Catholic ecclesiology. That church regards Peter as the first bishop of Rome and the first in a succession of popes continuing to the present day. Protestant scholars, to whom this is anathema, suggest that it is Peter's faith that is being rewarded here, not Peter himself. That is a difficult argument to sustain. However, there is certainly no suggestion that Peter is being appointed the first of many. Whatever is being awarded to Peter is awarded to him alone. He is always mentioned first in lists of apostles, and Acts records the part he played in the establishment of the early Church.

The word *ekklesia* is only used by Matthew among the Gospel writers (cf. 18.17). It is usually translated 'church', though there has been a great deal of reading back into that designation from later experience, as to what exactly 'church' might mean in that context. Matthew's church seems particularly undeveloped. The only possible office bearers mentioned are scribes (surely demanded by the continual references to 'their' scribes), prophets and righteous men (10.41). There are liturgical allusions which we have noted, and which may belong to a later time, but we should be cautious as we try to picture the church for which this Gospel is intended. The Greek word simply means 'crowd', 'congregation' or 'community'. The motif of building on rock has already been employed (7.24–7), but elsewhere in the New Testament it is Christ who is described as the cornerstone, usually in the context of a quotation from Psalm 118.22 about the cornerstone having been rejected. 1 Peter employs the building metaphor to memorable effect as the author describes the congregation as 'living stones' built on Christ the foundation stone. This is a possible example of the new temple motif traceable to Ezekiel and popular with one strand of messianic expectation, and that may also play a part in Matthew's description here.

Matthew goes on to describe Peter's role in more detail. Jesus will give him the keys of the Kingdom of Heaven and will give him authority to bind and to loose. Some see this as a later addition, but it need not be so. A Messiah needs a community. To say that the gates of Hades (i.e. death) will not prevail against it is perhaps to say no more than that it will not be killed off. Whatever being given the keys means, it surely cannot mean that Peter is being admitted to the kind of role that the rest of the Gospel has been railing against. Jesus describes this as 'my' community, and France concludes, 'So Peter is to be the foundation-stone of Jesus's new community of the restored people of God, a community which will last forever' (France 1985, p. 259), and perhaps that is as much as the evidence would definitely support. France believes that the image of the keys belongs less to the gatekeeper than the steward, the administrator, who had the power to make decisions, to allow or forbid. In case he, or the reader, should gain too high an estimate of him, he is immediately slapped down for his misunderstanding of what the Messiah role involves in terms of suffering. This should have come as no surprise, because it formed part of the charge to the apostles in chapter 10 (10.38–9). In 16.23 he describes Peter as a *skandalon*, Jesus's most biting term of abuse. Jesus is prepared to describe Peter as 'blessed' (16.17, *makarios*), on account of God's revelation to him about Jesus; but especially blessed are those who are not scandalized by Jesus (11.6). This word group, not always recognized in English translation, is used by Matthew at least 14 times. It is his favourite word for those who cannot accept his message, and who cause others to sin. We are left, here, with an ambiguous picture of the place of Peter in Jesus's estimation. It's an ambiguous picture that, ironically, makes Peter a more attractive figure in Rowena's eyes.

To do

An emerging question is about whether Jesus intended to form a church. Which of these statements best sums up how you see things at this point? Are they mutually exclusive?

- Jesus did intend to form a church. It was to be a reformed version of the Jewish religion system.
- Jesus did intend to form a church, but that was to be something radically different from the Jewish religious system.
- Jesus was only concerned for the Kingdom and did not intend to form a church.
- Jesus wanted the Church to foreshadow the Kingdom in some way.
- Some other interpretation.

What do you think are the implications for each of those views? Check this again at the end of the chapter.

Chapter 17 of the Gospel has three sections. The first describes what has come to be called the Transfiguration (literally *metamorphosis*), which appears in each of the Synoptic Gospels. Matthew has made a number of small alterations to Mark's account, the most significant of which appears to be that the disciples are afraid after they hear the voice of God, rather than initially. This provokes a word of reassurance from Jesus: 'do not be afraid'. Much of what can be said about this account could be said about the parallels in Mark and Luke, which are worth comparing, but from Matthew's account we could certainly say:

- This is an occasion when God is wonderfully and majestically present. The account is redolent with Old Testament images of presence, including the light, the brightness, the whiteness and the cloud.
- Following Old Testament precedent, speaking to God leads to a brightness of face (Exodus 34.33–5).
- The full transcript of what God said mirrors exactly what was said at Jesus's baptism. Both affirmations lead to vocational paths being followed, despite temptations to the contrary (26.39).
- The group of disciples that accompanies Jesus on the mountain is the same as accompanies him in Gethsemane (26.37).

- Peter (as in the other Gospels) is the leader and spokesman.
- This is the key turning-point in the narrative which now points towards Jerusalem and death.
- From this point the disciples do believe that Jesus must suffer (17.23b). In Mark the emphasis is on the Resurrection, and simply leads to discussion (Mark 9.10), and in Luke there is a complete lack of comprehension among the disciples (Luke 9.45).
- The command to silence (the last in this Gospel) only extends until 'the Son of Man had been raised from the dead' (17.9).

Following the descent from the mountain there is a healing miracle. Characteristically, this abbreviates Mark's account and focuses attention on a saying of Jesus – in this case on the importance of faith (cf. 8.13, 9.22, 15.28) and as a comment on discipleship. One is left with a sense that Jesus's reassurance and his emphasis on having and maintaining faith are the elements that might strike an initial audience most forcibly. The final section of the chapter is peculiar to Matthew and describes the tax inspectors making enquiries about whether Jesus pays the half-shekel temple tax. It is Peter who says that he does. Since Jesus has no money or possessions an improbable miracle provides the cash.

To do

Although this incident seems like an after-thought following the lofty theology that has gone before, it does raise a legitimate and practical question about discipleship. Should Jesus pay to support a regime in the temple with which he has substantial disagreement? Can you think of examples from more recent history where people have refused to pay tax on conscientious or religious grounds. What is your view of that? How would you read this passage in the light of your answer?

The climax of the section is the fourth discourse, so called, in chapter 18. Its content includes sayings, parables and references to forgiveness and disciplinary procedures which commentators take to be a description of how churches should live, and their members relate. Minear calls it A Manual of Discipline (pp. 100ff), Hill, The Life and Discipline of the Christian Community (pp. 272ff), and Hare, Life Together in the Church (pp. 208ff). The willingness to use the term 'Church' here is prompted by the use of the term *ekklesia* at 18.17. As noted above, this probably means Matthew's congregation and does not presuppose something with a developed or structured organization.

Let us consider what we already have learned from Matthew about the Church. By implication we have learned quite a lot about how a religious community should *not* work. It should not be hierarchical. It should not be obsessed by rules and laws. It should not confer authority on gatekeepers who can abuse their power. On the other hand, it should be a community that mirrors or embodies Kingdom values. Among other things, that means paying attention to the least. It should be a context in which people can show their best side. It should have a mission mentality. It should be a community that has a real sense of God's reassuring presence and help, despite possible hardship and suffering. Its priorities should be those of Jesus himself, namely preaching, teaching and healing, and especially teaching. Healing involves forgiveness.

We have already learned something about Matthew's own community from the special M material in chapter 13, with the parable of the wheat and the tares. Matthew's church is mixed in several senses. It has questions about doctrinal purity, about the place of Jewish converts and, by implication, the place of judgement. The worst thing to be is a *skandalon*, a stumbling block to others. In chapter 16 we had further information about authority and its implementation. It makes sense to talk about 'entry' into the Kingdom. The way in is narrow. There are entry requirements but they are not coextensive with those of old religious communities. Peter, either individually or in a representative capacity, holds the administrative keys. Chapter 18 gives practical resolution and illustration to some of these characteristics.

The chapter begins with a question prompted by Mark's account of a dispute among the disciples (Mark 9.34–7), about who is the greatest. Children exemplify true greatness (18.1–5). And Christians should avoid being a stumbling block to them at all costs (vv 6–10). They are to be nurtured. This appears to have become a reference to more than children. 'The least' means any vulnerable person. These people should not be lost as the parable of the lost sheep demonstrates. Luke tells the same parable but with a different meaning – the joy of finding a lost sinner. Matthew tells the story in the context of keeping the whole community together and giving especially the most vulnerable members a real sense of worth.

Verses 15–20 describe the procedure for dealing with a member who sins against another member. 'This is as close as we come in Matthew to an actual handbook of rules for the community' (Hagner 1993, vol. 2, p. 530). This is followed by a question about forgiveness, the answer to which includes a parable and a final statement about the importance of forgiving the brother from the heart (18.35). France considers this to be an extended commentary on Luke 6.36: 'If the church is the community of the forgiven, then all its relationships will be marked by a forgiveness which is not a mere form of words but an essential characteristic' (France 1985, p. 281).

The fact that this teaching on forgiveness comes last emphasizes its importance. The rest of the discourse might be seen in the light of this teaching.

The important thing is to keep the community together. That is achieved by attention to the least and to good relations between everyone. 'The community must treat its members as God treats them' (Hagner 1993, p. 541).

In this section Rowena has seen her initial interest in Peter as a character connecting the Church of the present to the Church of the past, expanding to include larger questions about the way the emerging Church was dealing with questions around structure and leadership and how discipleship managed to still have a central place.

To do

Go back to your discussion about whether Jesus intended to found a church. Has the subsequent discourse changed anything for you? If you believe that it is inevitable that Jesus should have a legacy, has Matthew judged it correctly, do you think?

6

Jesus: The End of
the Beginning

Veronika started going to church when she arrived in the UK from the Czech Republic a few years ago, as a student. She had been brought up under a Communist regime and so was surprised that some of her new friends should find church-going so important in their lives. Veronika loves her new life. She loves the sense of belonging to a loving community. She loves the gentleness she encounters in the people she has come to know, which contrasts with much that was more aggressive in her old life. One Sunday she was quite disturbed by one line in a hymn they sang: 'On the cross as Jesus died, the wrath of God was satisfied.' This seemed to counter her whole view of God, and even perhaps of the basis of the community she has come to trust. She has begun to ask questions that had not occurred before, and in particular: why did Jesus come, and why did he have to die? As the first book in the New Testament is Matthew's Gospel, she has decided to look for answers there. With the help of scholarship on the Gospel, she has begun to see what scholarship can contribute to her understanding of this basic issue. What she has found initially is that scholars often describe the first three Gospels as 'Passion Narratives with an introduction'. What she understands by that is that the question she is asking, why did Jesus die, is the question they are trying to answer, but that the first part of each Gospel sets a context in which the answer to the main question makes any sense. In other words, it's not just a story about a cross but about a whole ministry that gives that cross its particular significance.

From her own experience, she relates that to a travel guide. Usually, a good deal of the book is concerned with facts and impressions about the country in practical terms that might be useful to a foreigner planning a visit. In addition, there is often a fairly lengthy section that isn't just concerned with where the buses go from or how you buy a ticket, but rather with understanding the country you're visiting from a number of perspectives: historical, geographical, political, contemporary social, and perhaps even one on cuisine.

She has come to see how Matthew's Gospel does something similar. The climax of the Gospel is a continuous narrative about the foundational events of Christianity. We think of this as the Passion Narrative, and it is introduced in chapter 21 with the account of Jesus's entry to Jerusalem.

But in addition to this central Passion Narrative we have an extended introduction in chapters 1–20, which invites us not just to know what Jesus did in the last week of his earthly life that Christians specially remember, but, like the travel guide, to understand the significance of it all, from a number of perspectives. One perspective is provided by the names that this man goes by. Another is provided by his attitude towards Judaism as a religious system. A third is provided by a retrospective series of allusions about his abiding legacy in a continuing community, and particularly what is meant and required by ongoing discipleship. A fourth perspective is that of world history, which we shall consider in the next chapter. In this chapter, we shall follow Veronika's journey of discovery as we consider what those first three perspectives have taught us about Jesus, and we shall see how they are concluded in chapters 19–22. Also, we shall see how that conclusion leads naturally to the narrative that follows, as the alternative that Jesus provides demonstrates a judgement on religion as practised, which is unbearable to those who hold power.

To do

Do you think this is a fair summary of the perspectives that Matthew is offering? Can you think of others?

We shall come to the Passion Narrative directly, but first, following the introduction of the Narrative in chapter 21, there are what appear to be some interruptions or excurses. The latter part of chapter 21 and all of chapter 22 read like a continuation of chapters 19 and 20. Then there are two interruptions with specific content. The first interruption is contained in chapter 23, with its diatribe against the Jewish religious leaders. The second is chapters 24 and 25. They form the final one of the five so-called discourses. Its subject is the end of the age (see below, Chapter 7). These sections form the conclusion of the 'perspectives'.

Let us first consider what we have learned so far. On **names**: we have been introduced to Jesus at the outset as the Messiah. The Messiah was the one expected to inaugurate the Kingdom of God. However, Jesus's Messiahship differs markedly from what people, especially religious Jewish leaders, expect; and his description of what the Kingdom means also differs from their expectation. Much of the Gospel so far has been about the Kingdom, and in these last few chapters before the Passion we get concluding stories and actions that are consistent with what has gone before, and which bring the presentation towards a climax. We are told also that the Messiah has two names from the outset. One is Emmanuel. This is the name of reassurance, repeated in the last verse of the Gospel, about God's abiding presence with his people no matter how great might be the evidence to the contrary. Faith consists to an extent in trusting that. The other name is Jesus, and from a culture in which names are descriptions, this name describes the Messiah's purpose in terms of salvation. It is a name which has not been a matter of controversy throughout the early chapters but whose force will become clear in this summing up, specifically at 20.28. We have become so accustomed to hearing the name, Jesus, throughout the Gospel that it may have escaped us that, like Emmanuel, 'Jesus' is not a name used to address him in the presumed historical context. It is used only by the author. Indeed the name is not used when it would seem most obvious to use it and when the alternative sounds rather clumsy or contrived. So in 11.2 we read that John sent his disciples to put a question to 'Christ'. The question is: are you Christ?(!) At 13.54 one might have expected the question to include the name Jesus, as in: who does Jesus think he is? The point of the name, which is known to the reader all along, will only become clear from 20.27 onwards. We might also note that a kingdom demands a king, and that is a title applied to Jesus, albeit ironically, at various places in the Passion Narrative proper (e.g. 27.11, 29, 37, 42).

Terms that are used to address 'the one the reader knows as Jesus' include Son of David and Son of Abraham. The latter is dismissed as a useful term as early as 3.9 and does not reappear. Son of David is used elsewhere to connect Jesus with Jewish culture, expectation and imagination. However, that too is used in unexpected ways. The Syro-Phoenician woman, who wants Jesus to heal her daughter, appears in the narrative in order to make a point about non-Jews, but ironically (and obviously on purpose) she addresses Jesus as Son of David (15.22; cf. 9.27, 12.23).

Jesus is addressed on a number of occasions as *Rabbi* or Jewish religious teacher (e.g. 8.19). *Rabbi* is the term generally used when speaking with disciples. For non-disciples, the author prefers the secular *didaskolos*, teacher (9.11, 12.38, 17.24, 19.16, 22.16, 24, 36). This tells us something about Matthew's priority in presenting Jesus as a teacher (cf. 4.23, 9.35, 28.20). From 3.17 onwards we have explicit evidence of what is implicit in 2.15, that the Jesus is Son of God. In this first instance that revelation leads immediately to the questioning by the devil, two of which questions begin: 'if you are the Son of God . . .' (4.3, 4.6). This designation is about Jesus, and it does not make an exclusive claim about God, who is addressed as Our Father (6.9) and later described as your Father (e.g. 6.18, 10.20). Demons recognize Jesus by this title (again ironically) at 8.29. Finally, the disciples recognize him in this term (14.33, 16.16). The more Hellenistic term of respect for a religious figure is *Kyrios*, and that is also used (e.g. 8.6, 8.8 on the lips of a Gentile, 8.21, 8.25 in a quasi-liturgical setting, 14.28, 30 from Peter, again in a quasi-liturgical context. At 16.22 Peter, having just described Jesus as Christ, addresses him still as *Kyrios*: 17.15; cf. 18.21.)

The oft-used self-designation of Jesus is Son of Man. Again, no one addresses Jesus in this way, but it is always how he describes himself in formal contexts. Clearly this is not self-explanatory because it still makes sense to ask, 'Who do people say that the Son of Man is?' (16.13). There is much debate about the use of the term in the apocalyptic tradition at the time of Jesus, the key exegetical focus being Daniel 7.13. In Hebrew the term could simply mean 'human being' as in, for example, Ezekiel 37.3. However, its use in Daniel 7.13 has led to speculation that a key role of a designated figure named the Son of Man is to bring the righteous before God (the Ancient of Days) for vindication at the end of the age. Matthew uses the term in some of his more apocalyptic moments (10.23, which apparently refers to a future event, even though Jesus is speaking; 12.40, 13.37, 16.27–8, etc.), but also in general descriptions (e.g. 8.20, 9.6, in claiming authority, cf. 12.8, 11.19, etc.). We shall consider this further in the next chapter.

The use of each of these titles has to be seen, in Matthew's Gospel, against the background of the literary construction he is attempting, that at once combines the earthly ministry of Jesus with his post-resurrection exaltation as Lord of the Church. This brings an inevitable tension, since the earthly ministry is characterized by lowliness and service, whereas the post-resurrection faith of the Church demands a risen Lord who is exalted and powerful. According to Raymond Brown, 'Matthew resolves some of the tension in the account of the public ministry taken over from Mark by allowing the exalted status of Jesus to break through the lowliness so that on certain occasions his disciples recognize who he is' (Brown 1994, p. 118). Among the passages Brown cites as evidence are: Matthew 14.23–33; cf. Mark 6.47–52; Matthew 16.13–23; cf. Mark 8.27–33; Matthew 9.22; cf. Mark 5.30–1. From the passages we are now considering: 'the withering effect of the cursing of the fig tree by the Markan Jesus does not become apparent until the next day (11.20–1), whereas the tree withers immediately when the Matthean Jesus curses it (21.19–20)' (Brown 1994, p. 120).

To do

Look through a modern hymn-book that includes hymns from ancient as well as modern sources, and see how the names given to Jesus have varied over the years. Do the names in Matthew's Gospel still have meaning today or do names like 'Lord of the Dance' or 'Servant King' have more resonance? Do the names we use for Jesus today reflect his lowliness or his majesty? Which do you prefer? What does your answer tell you about your own 'Christology'? Do you feel the Gospel gives us permission to be inventive?

On **relations with Judaism,** there are some mixed messages. This is clearly the Gospel that makes the most of traditional Jewish religious language. Its arguments rely on Old Testament proof texts and the stated mission is to the lost sheep of the house of Israel (10.6, 15.24). It is the God of Israel who is praised (15.31). Jesus has come not to abolish the law and prophets but to fulfil them (5.17, where the reference to prophets is often overlooked). If France is correct in his view that the key theme of the Gospel is fulfilment (France 1985, p. 41), that demands a special status for the tradition in which expectation was fostered. On the other hand, this is the Gospel which is most vehement about the way in which religious professionals have subverted the original intention of the law and the prophets. From the outset they are described as a vipers' brood (3.7, 12.34), who can salvage no security from either claiming that they are children of Abraham (3.9) or from being familiar with liturgy (7.21, though this may have wider reference). It is the religious establishment that challenges Jesus and is suspicious of him (e.g. 12.1–13, 22–4). It is the leaven of the Pharisees that is to be avoided (16.11–12). The condemnation of Jewish teachers in chapter 23 is peculiar to Matthew. 'It must be recognized that in its present form, chapter 23 is a piece of religious polemic, created not by Jesus but by the author of the Gospel' (Hare 1993, p. 264). It is important, as scholars generally acknowledge, to locate what Matthew says about Judaism within his context, and not as evidence for a modern form of anti-Semitism. It is generally assumed that Matthew's own congregation is a mixture of Jews and Gentiles, and struggling with a new concept of religion that in a sense disregards nationality.

Every accusation that is levelled against the Pharisees and Sadducees has implications for what the **community of disciples** should be and do. Although there are continuities – the same continuities that allow Christians today to regard the Old Testament as sacred scripture – there are radical differences. They include the way followers of Jesus should interpret religious law. Other new interpretations involve hierarchies, the use and abuse of power, the dignity accorded to vulnerable 'little ones', and structures that discourage self-righteousness. Disciples must recognize their reliance on God's grace; must trust him even in difficult times; must be persistent in mission; must train to be reliable teachers; must maintain a teaching and healing ministry; and they must accept the out-of-comfort-zone revelation without being scandalized. Most recently in the Gospel we have learned that disciples must take up a cross and be prepared to suffer.

At the same time there is some ambiguity about the relation between the Church and the Kingdom. Are they co-extensive? The answer will depend on the extent to which we, the reader, believe the Kingdom is a present reality, or whether we believe it is mostly a future aspiration. Whatever the answer to that (see next chapter for further discussion), clearly the ongoing community must espouse, and try to embody, Kingdom norms. This must be a community in which the smallest are greatest, the first last, the non-Jews join with prostitutes and tax collectors in an inclusive society which is characterized by love of the least.

To do

Veronika regards this as a fair summary of what Matthew is telling us about Jesus and his intentions up to the end of chapter 18. Do you agree with her?

It would be helpful at this point to read Matthew chapters 19 and 20, 21.28–45 and chapter 22.

In chapters 19 and 20 we find that in each of the categories mentioned above we have the last word before the main event of the Passion, beginning with the community of faith, and what is asked of its members. Paul Minear notes the precise audience for each of Jesus's sayings in this section. He believes there is a pattern in which an issue raised by non-disciples provides an opportunity for further teaching to those who raise the issue, but that there is an additional piece of teaching for the disciples in each case (Minear 1984, pp. 104ff). He believes it important to note that distinction. The first example is the teaching on divorce (19.3–9). This is a further opportunity to use the same kind of method of exegesis we have already seen in the Sermon on the

Mount. The intention of God the creator was that man and woman should become one flesh. Those divorced and remarried are effectively adulterers. Faced with what Moses 'commanded' (19.7), Jesus points out that Moses did not command it but tolerated it as a concession to human hardness of heart, though Matthew does admit one exception – unchastity, *porneia* (usually taken to mean unfaithfulness, cf. 5.32). This is followed by teaching specific to the disciples. This is sometimes interpreted as Jesus stating that celibacy is better than marriage, but that would surely conflict with what he has just said to the Pharisees about the God-given gift of marriage to humankind. Minear believes that this provides an occasion when the disciples are encouraged to think most seriously about their vocation and the sacrifices it might mean. In this interpretation we see the same basic method as in the great sermon. Jesus's appeal is to first principles, 'in the beginning' (19.4, 8). 'An ethic that is truly to reflect God's will must be built, not on concessions but on basic principles' (France 1985, p. 284).

The next brief episode (vv 13–15) does not show Jesus addressing the crowds, but his action is in a sense a form of address. The children are brought to him to be blessed and the disciples rebuked them. They themselves are rebuked by Jesus. This is a reminder of what Jesus has said about the importance of the 'little ones' and perhaps also that only those who become like children will enter the Kingdom (18.3). This might also remind us (as it does Minear) of other occasions when Jesus shows compassion towards children, especially when their parents intercede for them (9.18–19, 17.15–16; Minear 1984, p. 105). He concludes that Jesus's teaching to the disciples was that 'The coming of the kingdom destroyed any idea of special privilege for any group, old or young, rich or poor, powerful or weak' (p. 105). It could be argued, surely, that actually the passage demonstrates a special privilege for the children, and by implication all included in the designation 'little ones'. Case-Winters sees a new inclusivity commended here, in a society in which children under the age of 12 had no status, and girls not even then. She notes that in the feeding miracles, specific mention is made of women and children (e.g. 14.21, 15.28; Case-Winters 2015, p. 240). Children also present a paradigm of help-less dependence (Hare 1993, p. 224). For all that, it would be consistent within the chapter for Matthew to be describing how his Church should operate.

Matthew 19.16–30 describes a dialogue with a rich man (whom Matthew alone describes as a *young* man) followed by a discussion with the disciples. This section is reminiscent of Jesus's conversation with Nicodemus in John 3.1–21 (so Hare 1993, p. 226). He also notes that the word used for the 'perfection' urged on the young man in Greek is *teleios*. In mod-ern Greek this would have the sense of 'complete' rather than perfect. Hare notes that this word trans-lates the Hebrew *shalem* at 1 Kings 11.4, where the meaning is probably something like 'at one with', but which Hare translates in terms of undivided devotion (Hare 1993, p. 227). These may seem rather detailed points but they would be of supreme interest to a community of disciples, or a Matthean Church community, wanting to know exactly what they have signed up for in terms of a complete lifestyle.

Minear's summary of this teaching is, 'Disciples can either debate what is impossible for human beings or celebrate what God has made possible' (1984, p. 106). What we might say is that the whole chapter deals with issues that affected the twelve, but also affected continuing leaders (and perhaps other members) of the early Church. Should they be married? This is still an issue in the world-wide Christian Church. This is closely followed by the issue of whether Church leaders should have property, possessions and money. Between them, the question raised is whether Christian leaders should lead 'normal' lives as members of their communities, like other people, or whether their chosen lifestyle should set them apart, either through sexual abstinence or by renouncing the normal securities of life. This continued to be an issue in the early Church, which eventually and uneasily arrived at a 'mixed economy' solution.

To do

What is your view on this issue? Should there be a very public demonstration of poverty and chastity on behalf of church leaders? Are these in any case the most desirable characteristics of leaders? Is it more important to show the 'normality' of Christian life in a way that allows the maximum number to identify with it? Is there a case to be made for monks and nuns? What should their relationship be with the church-in-the-community?

Chapter 20.1–28 is also addressed to the disciples. Minear believes that it addresses the issue of whether second-generation leaders are less important than the original disciples. Actually, though, the passage follows discussion about the rewards that disciples can expect and so might naturally be thought to relate to that precise issue. In that case it would have something to say about the grace of God; the fact that humans do not set the rules for the Church (20.15), and that we cannot present God with a bill for services rendered, in the way of normal human transactions. Christian service has to be within a relationship that is something more than transactional. The number of conclusions to the parable might reflect later Church accretions (so Minear 1984, p. 108, who sees four 'punchlines' in vv 13–16), in which case that would bear witness to the liveliness of the issue within the early Church and the different emphases placed by a different reading of it. Although there is clear reference to the Church suggested by the link with the preceding section, the parable begins, 'The Kingdom of Heaven is like . . .', maintaining the ambiguity noted.

Hagner draws attention to the reason why the last group employed had not started work earlier, 'because no-one has hired us' (20.7). As with any selection method, be it for a sports team at school, or workers under an old system on the dockside, the most able would be chosen first and the ones left would be the least capable, the old, sick, unskilled etc. The real scandal of the story for him is that these are invited to join the work party and treated equally with the rest (Hagner 1993, p. 571). In his view, allegorically they are equivalent to the harlots and tax collectors invited into the Kingdom by Jesus.

Hare regards this parable as similar to that of the Prodigal Son. This parable occurs only in Matthew: the latter only in Luke. In each case, the one who apparently deserves most is overlooked in favour of the one who apparently deserves least. However, he believes the different authors use these stories in different ways.

A further consideration is whether the scene described in 19.28 is the context in which we must read this parable. Is it in fact a parable about the last judgement, when 'the Son of Man is seated on his glorious throne' (cf. 25.31)? Senior, for example, assumes that because so many labourers are being hired, this must be harvest time, with all that that implies in terms of images of judgement (cf. 13.30; Senior 1998, p. 222). Fenton believes that the Church has taken a parable of Jesus, originally about ministry, and used it as a parable of judgement (1963, p. 319). It is difficult to sustain the argument that this is a judgement parable. There is no action of division, which characterizes other examples of judgement. It is more likely that the message is about grace and God's surprises. Though, confronted with attitudes such as those employed by the sons of Zebedee and their mother in the succeeding passage, some element of judgement is implied.

Verse 20.28 is a key one. Veronika feels that this is where she might find the answer to her anxiety about singing the hymn that prompted her enquiries. For Hare, 'with this statement concerning the significance of Jesus's death, the extended introduction has reached its goal' (Hare 1993, pp. 235–6). This certainly sums up succinctly the massive cultural difference between Christian ministry and that of the Jewish religious leaders. The one is about being powerful gatekeepers and, if you like, being the masters of the people. Christian ministry is about being servants to the people. They follow the example of the Son of Man and must indeed be more than servants. They must be slaves. This narrative is given practical demonstration in the foot-washing in John's Gospel 13.14–17. The word 'ransom' has been the basis of some theories of atonement (i.e. what Jesus *achieved* on the cross). The rationale for this is made by connecting 1.21 where Jesus is named, with 20.28. The basic thesis is that in order either to satisfy the wrath of God about sin, or to rescue perishing souls from the grasp of Satan who has caused them to sin, a ransom is necessary, and it is Jesus who pays with his life.

This is not assumed in the text, where the chief focus is on the attitude to ministry. There are probably echoes here also of the servant song in Isaiah 53. But there is no escaping the term 'ransom'. Whether 'give his life' assumes death and martyrdom, or whether an interpretation along the lines of 'dedicate his life sacrificially' might be more in keeping with the context, the fact remains that Christian tradition has used the saying to connect with 1.21 and to see this as the ultimate description of Jesus's mission. No clear link is made, either, between this passage and the Kingdom, which was Jesus's own description of his mission and the one he urged his disciples to maintain (10.7). Some scholars regard the second half of the verse as a later addition by the Church which was seeking to make sense of Jesus's death. The fact that the verb 'came' is in the aorist tense is sometimes cited as evidence. However 26.28, Jesus's words at the Last Supper, is consistent with what is assumed by scholars here. This is the only other place in the Gospel where there is a rationale for Jesus's death spoken by Jesus himself. What should not be missed in either of these sayings is that this is not just an ontological kind of statement, but one that has practical effect. And that effect leads to some kind of liberation. Hare believes that the metaphor of ransom should not be pressed to the point where we ask to whom the ransom should be paid. He notes that in Jeremiah 31 the idea of ransom is paralleled by that of redemption. Both are metaphors with more traction in their times than ours. 'The saying in Matthew 20.28 does not explain the mystery of the atonement but simply affirms the fact of Christian experience that in and through Jesus Christ, our rebellion against our creator has been overcome' (Hare 1993, p. 235).

To do

Do you think Veronika's questions, what did Jesus come for? and why did he have to die? are answered? Think about how you would answer them after reading Matthew's Gospel to this point. What more do we need to know?

This final section of the 'perspectives' includes three parables which could be taken as a response to the challenge to Jesus's authority as set out at 21.23–7.

The first concerns two sons (21.28–32). One says he will do the father's bidding but does not. The second says that he will not do the father's bidding but changes his mind and does it. The form of the story, which is told to those who challenge him, is interesting, in that it invites an initial response which then is used against the responders.

Jesus asks: 'which of the two sons did the father's will?' and the 'chief priests and elders of the nation' reply that the second did. Jesus then turns this on them, and repeats his familiar refrain that tax collectors and prostitutes will enter the Kingdom before these people who failed to heed the words of John.

The second is an extended allegory (21.33–46). This is a story of wicked tenants who try to take the vineyard by force from the rightful owner. They kill his son, and as a result the owner gives the vineyard to others who will act as tenants should, and give the owner what is due to him. This appears to widen the scope of the story from the immediate context to the wider one of all who reject the teaching of Jesus and John. The vineyard would be given to another 'nation'. The Greek word *ethnos* is used. When used in the plural this usually refers to Gentiles, but in the singular, that is not so. Jesus is not saying that the Kingdom will be taken from Jews and given to Gentiles. Rather, he appears to be referring to 'religious nations'. The Kingdom will cease to be the preserve of the Jews and will henceforth be the gift to the Christian Church. In other words, the question is: who are the real people of God? This theme of the rejection of official Israel is a more pronounced theme in Matthew than the other Gospels.

The third parable is about a wedding feast (22.1–14). Commentators see the parallel in Luke 14.15–24 as being an earlier version of the parable (so also Gospel of Thomas 64). In both cases this is a straightforward story about God's gracious invitation being treated lightly, with the result that the feast instead will feature outcasts: the poor, the crippled, blind and lame. The point here is that Jesus accepts the outcasts who do respond to him. Matthew's version is far more involved, may involve further layers of Church accretion (with a possible allusion to the fall of Jerusalem 22.7), and has been altered to a point where it becomes quite ludicrous. The suggestion is that this has been adapted to describe the whole history of salvation and to match 21.33–43. The final saying of Jesus acts as a commentary on all three parables: many are invited but few are chosen (22.14).

To do

Bearing in mind all that has been said, read chapter 23. What do you think is its main message?

All of this builds towards chapter 23, and the denunciation of the religious leaders. Jesus is the true heir. The Church is the true heir of Jesus. That Church will be mixed. It will include Jews and Gentiles, good and bad (22.10), it will be led by those who 'understand' and will consist of those who have responded to the invitation. Israel, it turns out, are not, after all, the elect. They are actually the called.

To do

Think about the last comment. What would you say are the main characteristics of those who think they are the elect, as opposed to those who think they are called?

7

Jesus: The Beginning of the End

Sue has been attending a study group at her local church, working through the Gospel of Matthew for several weeks. She has tried, without success, to interest her husband Derek in the course. Derek attends church occasionally, mostly – if he were honest – to support his wife, but is rather dismissive of what he thinks of as the rather primitive assumptions of the Gospel context. His professional life is as a maths teacher in a local comprehensive school and his extra-mural interests are mostly concerned with science in some form. For example, he is a member of his local astronomy group, and is an avid reader of science fiction. Both Sue and Derek share concerns about the state of the world, and Sue is convinced that Derek will find the part of the Gospel her group is now approaching interesting, both from a moral and a scientific perspective. Derek agrees to come along, albeit reluctantly, to something he believes will be outside his comfort zone, to find that the discussion this week centres on Matthew chapters 23–5, which he reads with a sinking heart.

The first part of the evening deals with chapter 23 and seems to Derek to be concerned with detail rather than substance. He assumes his detachment is due to the fact that he has not been part of the group until now, and he listens patiently. It seems that there is some dispute about whether Matthew chapter 23 is a separate discourse, or whether it is part of the discourse that follows in chapters 24 and 25. Those who want to have a tidy five-fold pattern would obviously consider the chapters as one discourse, in which case the overriding theme would be one of judgement. Chapter 23 is about judgement on the scribes and Pharisees of Judaism. Chapters 24 and 25 widen the scope to speak of the last judgement at the end of the age.

There are good reasons to resist this interpretation (see Hagner 1993, pp. 654–5 for a full discussion). Chapter 23 could more properly be seen as the climax of the preceding section. It includes main themes, found elsewhere in the Gospel, that are summarized here in a dramatic polemic. They include:

- Israel has forfeited its right to any Kingdom privilege.
- One of the reasons is that Jewish teachers have failed to interpret the scriptures adequately (cf. John 5.39–40, 8.37–40).
- Jewish religious leaders have misunderstood and abused the power they have.

- Jewish religious leaders have misinterpreted devotional life – for example, the making of oaths.
- There is an aside to Christian leaders (23.8–12) not to follow their example.

Sue is quite at home in this discussion and is happy to participate in the group activity.

To do

See if you can find supporting evidence elsewhere in the Gospel for the claim that the points noted above are substantial themes in the Gospel of Matthew. Can you find other main themes represented in this chapter?

Derek has seen his interest flicker into life somewhat at the mention, in the discussion, of anti-Semitism. He notes that it is not the Jews as a whole (as compared with the Gospel of John) who are condemned, but the religious leaders, who, in a sense, could stand for the religious leaders in other religions at a variety of historical junctures. Indeed, it is possible to read the chapter as essentially addressed as a warning to Christian leaders rather than a diatribe against Jewish ones. 'Its purpose is to warn Christians against an attitude to God which is not impossible within the Church, and among disciples. The scribes and Pharisees are used as lay-figures, or representatives of practical atheism which masquerades as piety' (Fenton 1963, pp. 364–5). This is, after all, a book addressed to Christians, not Jews, but may include some apologetic purpose to help explain why the Jewish converts did the right thing in converting.

There is scholarly discussion about Matthew's source for this chapter which contains much original material. Particularly there is doubt about whether the passage is a Matthean creation designed to fit his situation, or whether the words do derive from Jesus (see above, Matthew 6).

To do

Re-read the chapter as addressed to Christian leaders nowadays. What would be appropriate within it, if anything? What might you rephrase in order to reflect current issues? Do you think that what is being said reflects Jesus's attitudes as expressed elsewhere?

The group then proceeds to chapters 24 and 25 which seem to Derek both more promising but more problematic. These chapters form the last universally recognized discourse in the Gospel. The early part of the discourse is based on the so-called 'Little Apocalpyse' of Mark chapter 13. Matthew has expanded on this material, substantially in chapter 24, and added much new material, peculiar to him, in chapter 25.

This is the absolute climax of the teaching prior to the Passion Narrative proper. The discourse introduces us to a raft of technical terms which were part of current theological discussion in Jewish religious culture. They derive from apocalyptic writing, though some had an earlier origin and reached their full development in apocalyptic thinking.

Apocalyptic writings were popular in Jewish culture for a period of around 400 years, from around 250 BCE/BC to CE/AD 150. They are modern, in the sense that they are overtly a written form rather than the reports of what was once spoken and they represent a fusion of two hugely important Old Testament theological strands. One of those is the Wisdom tradition. This is in turn based on the creation theology that sees order and purpose in the world. God as creator had definite intentions for the world, and foresaw a definite destiny for it. He ordered not only the various realms of nature, but also human society. This is big picture stuff and foresees, in addition to this, that God had devised an ordering of history that sees time divided into definite ages. To this, the prophetic tradition adds the belief that life also has a moral purpose which it articulates in terms of the Covenant ideas of justice and judgement.

The context in which this fusion works best is one of oppression and undeserved suffering. Effectively, the voice of faith asks: if God created the world so carefully, why do bad things happen to good people, and if there really is justice in the world, why do bad people not get their just deserts? The apocalyptic tradition says: justice will be meted out in the judgement at the end of the age, and in fact the end of the age is coming soon, so hang on in faith. This age will be followed by a new age in which all the design faults or design corruptions and subversions of this age will be resolved.

The tradition surfaces at a time when Jews (as we can now call them) felt hugely vulnerable, and as if their whole culture and identity was under threat. There were enemies on every side – the great empires of Greece and Rome – and they were a small remnant with memory of a God who had promised them, hundreds of years ago, that it would not come to this. They would have a land, they would have descendants and be a nation with which God would have a special relationship. God now seems very distant. His voice is not heard. Their experience is at odds with a faith they struggle to maintain. The pastoral message of the writings, which are very varied in their form, is to maintain faith despite everything. If the people do not succumb to idolatry or immorality, then they will finally be vindicated. All this is guaranteed – locked in to the plan of creation which is now unfolding.

This is both a literary and theological genre, and it has its own stylistic traits as well as its own technical vocabulary, and theological ideas. Some of these are well exemplified in the final Matthean teaching discourse, but will also be recognized from random allusions in the rest of the Gospel. A special area of interest concerned the way in which one age would give way to the next. There would be definite signs of the end. Just as human birth-giving was at the time painful, but gave way to something joyful, so the signs of the birth of the new age could be described as 'birth pangs' (Matthew 24.8) and could involve disruption, violence and suffering. However, these would be short lived and the expectation of the joy to come would mitigate their effect. The process clearly depended upon an initiative of God.

His anointed (Messiah or Christos) would be the agent of this initiative. In some traditions, he is described as war-like and leading an army. Others are less clear, but certainly he will bring about a great judgement, will proclaim the new Kingdom (or perhaps more properly, kingship of God – this is an active concept). He will pronounce a forgiveness which will make possible the new community. This is sometimes described as an 'eschatological' forgiveness (see Gowan 2000, pp. 59–60). This is a kind of final forgiveness which is necessary to transform the human person so as to make future forgiveness unnecessary, and which is unavailable at the human level. 'Eschatological' derives from the Greek word for last or final. It can refer to time (the end of the age), or to a person (Christ as the finality of humanness, the 'last' person, the *eschatos* (Revelation 1.17)). Gowan expresses it thus: 'the appearance in eschatological texts of promises of forgiveness and of the recreation of humanity so that no further occasions of forgiveness would ever arise reveals an underlying sense of the inadequacy of the restorative powers of forgiveness in the present' (Gowan 2000, p. 60).

The final consummation of the age will involve a general resurrection of the dead (Daniel 12.2). Hence New Testament reference to resurrection is not just a description of something that happened or will happen. It is a sophisticated reference that connects what happened or will happen to a whole tradition and expectation.

This brief sketch cannot do justice to what is a very complex network of ideas and idioms, but this is the religious cultural framework which many believe obtained in the first half of the first century, and which has given to the Gospel proclamation generally in the New Testament, both a vocabulary and an ethos. Matthew's Gospel is the one that most wholeheartedly embraces it.

Derek has found this fascinating, and in his own mind has been thinking about the similarities between apocalyptic and science fiction. Both seem to have a deep moral purpose, worked out against the background of the scientific knowledge of their age, complete with super heroes. On the other hand, Sue is struggling to connect this section with the rest of the Gospel.

To do

Looking back through the Gospel, where can you find evidence of this way of thinking? You might

> start with John's disciples' questions in 11.3.
> Chapter 13 has a number of examples, but there
> are far more. See what you can find.

Matthew 11.3 seems to suggest that Jesus is to be
identified with 'the one who is to come' – that is,
the inaugurator of the Kingdom. Matthew's identification of Jesus as the Messiah from the outset sets
a central theme of the Gospel. However, 24.3 reads
as if none of this had taken place. Here there is reference to the end of the age and Jesus's 'coming' as
if it were a totally future event. Signs are asked for
and given (contra 16.1–4, 12.38–40). These are not
signs of healing and forgiveness such as described
elsewhere in the Gospel, but rather signs of suffering, violence and destruction. The Greek word for
'coming' used here is *parousia*, a term which only
Matthew, among the Gospel writers, uses (24.3, 27,
37, 39). Most scholars want to retain this as a technical term without finding an exact equivalent for
it. Its literal meaning is 'being at hand' or 'presence'
(cf. 2 Corinthians 10.10). Not until the middle of
the second century is it used by Justin Martyr to
describe a 'second coming'.

The puzzling thing is that at this point scholars do
not find any of this odd. Indeed, for some, it is as if they
are reading into Matthew's account theological ideas
they have picked up from the early epistles of Paul,
as if they can be seamlessly applied. Fenton (1963)
heads this section, 'The End of the World' (p. 378).

That is clearly incorrect. What Matthew describes is the 'close of the age' (another phrase peculiar to him (cf. 13.39, 40, 49, 28.20). Hagner describes the chapter as dealing with the *eschaton* (1993, p. 690). This is a word that never occurs in the New Testament in the singular as if to signify a final event. In any case, Matthew uses *telos* to describe the end. As Hill points out, this does not mean the End, but rather 'finally' (Hill 1972, p. 321, in reference to 24.13). France tells us that the word *parousia* is used in secular literature to describe 'official visits by high-ranking persons', and so is appropriate for an 'ultimate visitation' (France 1985, p. 340). Commenting on Matthew 24.37, Hagner speaks of the 'return' of the Son of Man even though his own translation simply uses *parousia* in the original Greek.

In the middle of the twentieth century, there was much interest in New Testament eschatology, and close examination of apocalyptic thinking and its technical terms. Two studies in particular, *The Second Advent* (Glasson 1947), and *Jesus and His Coming* (Robinson 1957), looked at how the doctrine of a second coming had emerged in the early Church, and questioned whether the Church had misunderstood the teaching of Jesus. These were written, it must be said, at a time when there was also great interest in how oral traditions had been communicated to the point where they reached the written sources of the Gospels, and what corruption and accretion or 'creativity' had taken place along the way, and there was special enthusiasm to discover that. With specific reference to eschatological themes, there had been great excitement at the publication of *The Parables of the Kingdom* by C. H. Dodd in 1935 (revised edition, Dodd 1961) and its claims that Jesus preached a 'realised eschatology' which did not demand a sequel. Robinson's own conclusion is that it would be better to speak of an inaugurated eschatology, begun by Jesus, and continuing, without the expectation of a second incarnation: 'the most profound expression of the truth, never lost in the New Testament, [is] that *parousia* is a word that has no plural. There is but one coming, begun at Christmas, perfected on the Cross, and continuing till all are included in it' (Robinson 1957, p. 185). The early Church had misunderstood Jesus, he believed, and had tried to postpone to a future date the judgement which Jesus's presence implied in the here and now.

If there was misunderstanding it occurred at a very early stage. Indeed scholars believe that part of chapter 24 is trying to deal with the fact that at the time of writing there was expectation of an imminent return of Jesus of the kind generated at Mark 9.1, and that it had not happened (24.37ff). But Matthew 24 appears to be lowering expectations of an imminent *parousia*; 24.4–8 is perhaps written to those who see in current cataclysmic events, whether natural or man-made disasters, signs of an impending end. The message is, there will always be such events. These are just the beginning. The Gospel has to be preached throughout the earth and to all nations before the end (*telos*) comes. That doesn't sound like any time soon. But the important thing is that there will be persecution in the short term and Christians must endure and believe in the long-term victory. This is a familiar theme in apocalyptic. The persistent message is that victory has been won and right and justice will win out over evil and power despite all the evidence to the contrary. The key thing is to resist immorality and idolatry, or, as Matthew says, to endure. Faith for these writers is not about believing that things happened. It is about trust in the promises, and trust in the relationship between God and his people that endures despite the evidence. In the meantime, those who claim to have evidence are to be treated with scepticism (24.23–6).

Derek's mind is working overtime now. He is coming to this not from a religious perspective but rather from the point of view of someone concerned about the environmental crisis in the world and so the world's sustainability. Could it be that the same kind of concern was to be found, of all places, in Matthew's Gospel? Sue, though, is still struggling. In the creed she says that Jesus will come again, and although she doesn't expect it to happen it gives her a sense of accountability for her actions. Has she really understood what is being said in the Gospel and has she got it all wrong?

In keeping with accepted scholarly practice in the twentieth century, the main interest in the Matthew 24 passage was in its provenance. Did it include original sayings of Jesus or was it a later addition from the Church, perhaps as a response to the destruction of Jerusalem in CE/AD 70? The source on which Matthew 24 is initially based is Mark 13. A long-standing theory, originated by Bishop Timothy Colani in the nineteenth century, was that this so-called 'Little Apocalypse' was a separate complete source (Mark 13.5–31) and that its use in the Gospels was quite discordant. In Mark's version, the disciples' question appears to be about the destruction of the Jerusalem Temple, rather than the end of the age. Matthew has readjusted it to give it a more universal scope. Other scholars have defended the authenticity of the eschatological discourses (e.g. Beasley-Murray 1954, 1993).

We might think that it would be helpful to compare Matthew 24 with current Jewish expectation, but in this instance that provides no clear picture. There was no Jewish expectation of a second Advent of the Messiah (2 Baruch 30). They never spoke of a/ the *parousia* of the Messiah. Daniel 7.13 is thought by many to be a key text from what would have been relatively recent apocalyptic writing, about the *parousia* of the Son of Man. Its distribution in contemporary theological thinking is, however, disputed, and in any case the text appears to describe a coming from earth to heaven and not the other way around, and there is ambiguity about whether the term 'Son of Man' is a definite title or a general description of a human being (see below). The text does point to a potentially useful distinction though.

In Daniel 7.13 'one like a son of man' coming with the clouds is described as approaching the 'Ancient of Years' in a theatrical scene in which the keynote is the vindication of the righteous, those who have kept faith (Daniel 7.18, 22). This raises the question whether the content of *parousia* doctrine is about visitation or vindication, and therefore whether Jesus's references to it, if they are authentic, have a temporal and literal sense or whether they offer yet one more perspective on his death. We have already seen how different temporal schemes, the time of Jesus and the time of the Church, are described together. It may be that the apocalyptic perspective is one more layer placed on top of all this to explain the more cosmic and universal significance of the crucifixion. In support of that view, Matthew does give the crucifixion an eschatological setting that other writers do not (Matthew 27.50–4), and introduces the Resurrection in apocalyptic terms that he has already used to describe the travails of the Church (28.2, cf. 8.24). *Parousia* belongs to a family of theological presentations that include resurrection, ascension and transfiguration. In John's Gospel all these appear to focus on, and be used to describe the significance of, the crucifixion; the moment of Jesus's glory. In Matthew's Gospel this is less clear and any of the possible theories may be correct.

To do

Colani wrote in 1874 that the second coming idea would make Jesus 'a humble and sweet precursor of a violent and terrible Messiah'. What is your reaction to this? Does this just reflect Victorian anxieties and romantic ideas of Jesus, or does he have a point? It is a very big step to say that the early Church misunderstood Jesus. What is your reaction to that suggestion? How do you think Derek and Sue might each react to it?

Chapter 24 does not have a single mention of the Kingdom of Heaven/God, but in the first verse of chapter 25 there is a seamless move that connects 'the day' with the Kingdom. In chapter 24 we might have been forgiven for thinking that Matthew had forgotten about his two main Christological themes: that Jesus is the Messiah, and that the Messiah inaugurates the Kingdom. This is surprising since Matthew uses the term 'Kingdom' far more than any other evangelist. He has 50 mentions as opposed to Mark's 14. There are 32 mentions of Kingdom in Matthew's special M material alone. What chapter 24 does provide us with, however, is further information about the Son of Man.

Burkett's summary of scholarship on this subject is not encouraging. 'Nineteen centuries of "Son of Man" study have led to no consensus concerning the meaning or origin of the expression. The Son of Man debate thus serves as a prime illustration of the limits of New Testament scholarship' (Burkett 1999, p. 5). The questions that are unresolved include the following.

- Did Jesus actually use the phrase as a self-designation, or is that a device of the evangelists or early Church?
- Why does the term only appear in the Gospels and not in the Epistles?
- Following Hebrew idiom, does this mean any more than human being (cf. Ezekiel 37.3, 9, 11, 15)?
- Is there an intended reference to Daniel 7.13?
- In the absence of clear evidence, did Daniel 7.13 feature in contemporary pre-Christian theological debate?
- If Jesus did use the phrase as a self-designation, did he use it cryptically (to conceal his identity), idiomatically (as a novel self-designation that had a degree of ambiguity), proleptically (to describe what he would be in the future) or scornfully (throwing back at opponents an epithet used against him)?
- Did Jesus revise his ideas about the Son of Man as his ministry moved into suffering mode, to include the tradition of the suffering servant?

This list is not exhaustive and these questions are not equally important, but they do give an indication of what Burkett was describing, and lead us to be cautious in expressing certainty in this area of theological debate. What we can say with certainty in reference to Matthew is that one role of the Son of Man is to be judge.

This has already been revealed in parables (13.40–1) and now other parables of judgement are presented. Chapter 25 includes the wise and foolish virgins (1–13), the use of talents (14–30) and the sheep and the goats (31–46). In each case judgement involves separation (as with the wheat and the weeds, and as we have just read in chapter 24.40–1). The first reminds us of the setting of the previous parable about a great banquet (22.1–14) and so sets the context as the Messianic feast at the end of the age. The message here is the theme of preparedness. In terms of discipleship, the message is do not take your eye off the ball and do not cease to believe in the potential presence of God. The word used for coming in v 10 is the usual descriptive word, and not a technical term.

The parable of the talents 'focuses on the responsibility of servants [disciples] to be about their master's work while he is "away"' (Hagner 1993, vol. 2, p. 732). Again, there seems to be an attempt to prepare disciples for the long term – 25.19 describes the master (*kyrios*) as being away 'for a long time'. In the act of giving the talent of the third servant who had done nothing with it but bury it, to the one who had been most entrepreneurial with his talent, there are echoes of the theme of giving to the Gentiles what had been entrusted to the Jews. But there is also the threat that Christians/disciples must themselves use what is entrusted to them, because that is the basis on which their discipleship will be judged. There is no privilege. That point is made most overtly in the third parable in the chapter: the sheep and the goats.

This is one of Sue's favourite stories from the Gospels and one she tries to apply to her own life as a Christian. She hopes it is not about to be undermined.

It is notable here that the judgement is on all the *nations* (25.32). Remember that this judgement will not happen (if we take the temporal allusion literally) until all the nations have heard the Gospel (24.14), so this is not just (as is sometimes said) a judgement on political systems and institutionalized sin, though there is no reason why that should be excluded, but it does describe judgement of individual actions. This parable is the most easily pictured in practical terms, and probably one of the most preached about. It encourages Christians to see Christ in the disadvantaged, the naked, hungry and homeless, and says that they will be judged, as we already realized from Jesus's previous references to the 'least', on their response to him as seen in the least. This is one of the most compassionate passages in the Gospels and takes us back to the realistic and practical concern that Matthew displayed in the great sermon, that Christian behaviour should display adult and mature and thought-through righteousness, and that it should value those generally disregarded by religious leaders unworthy of the title.

Derek sees the key to making a link with his own experience, what is meant by 'the end of the age'. If that is little more than saying 'in the last analysis' in a first-century kind of way, then he would find it easier to identify with. Those familiar with Old Testament traditions would have been expecting a judgement at the end of the age that would have 'righted wrongs'. This was the effect of the prophetic strand in apocalyptic thought. From a Jewish point of view this would have involved a punishment of those who had persecuted Jews, and the vindication of those who had 'endured' as a remnant, either as per Daniel 7.13 or in terms of a celebration in a messianic feast. What is being described here is quite different, though those traditions are alluded to. Here there is no privilege for Jews, and indeed not for Christians. The only criterion is love of the least.

To do

Think about what the terms 'judgement' and 'last judgement' mean to you. Do you think they occur at the end of the age, at a second coming of Christ, or perhaps at our own death? Is it always a future possibility? Alternatively, how does God's judgement work, if at all, in the present?

In this chapter we have dealt with what many would regard as some of the most difficult passages in the Gospel to relate to our own time and culture. Two of Fenton's six difficulties for the twentieth-century reader (Fenton 1963, pp. 17ff) appear specifically in this section. They are the imminent end of the world, and issues around rewards and punishments. Fenton's attempts to explain the former in terms of 'an integrated life' and 'wholeness' appear lame and desperate (p. 22). His analysis of rewards and punishments is more convincing. He believes that Christianity is never disinterested; that 'God's rewards are always greater than men's [sic] deserts' (p. 25), and that the rewards are designed for those who do what they do with no thought of reward.

On 'the imminent end of the world [sic]', what we actually see is a kind of tension between two things that Matthew may want to say. The first is that the present moment is one where decisive action is called for. People need to decide in favour of Jesus. In their everyday and recognizable life they need to be aware that their every action is significant and is under the judgement of God. He who is not with us is against us (12.30), and the crisis is now. We must decide which side of the dividing line we are on. On the other hand, we see a damping down of speculation about the end. People are obviously getting excited about current events: famines, warfare and perhaps the destruction of the Jerusalem Temple. They are told in effect: 'you ain't seen nothing yet'. These are the kinds of event that you could report at any time in the last 2,000 years in that region. What this suggests is that readers are not being invited to piece together some kind of temporal scheme, but rather to understand the content and rationale of

God's judgement which is foreshadowed and pro-leptically active in the present. This fits with the 'inaugurated' theme detected elsewhere. The signifi-cance of the Kingdom and of judgement is described in terms which reassure readers that the world does have a destiny and moral purpose, but it starts and is active now and not just in the future. The cruci-fixion is both the end of the age and the beginning of the end of all ages.

To do

What do you think Derek and Sue might talk about as they walk home? What understandings might they have in common? What have been the main challenges to faith, as they each under-stand it, and what might have changed for them through their participation in the group on that evening?

8

Ends and Beginnings

Phoebe's grandchildren are coming to stay for Easter. It is a matter of great regret to her that her own children have not followed her own active devotion to Christianity, and that has been compounded by her suspicion that her young teenage grandchildren are quite religiously illiterate. This year she intends to go to church as she always has during Holy Week and Easter itself. She intends to take the children with her and wants to prepare them for what they are going to hear. This is her opportunity to translate the fundamental message of the Gospel into terms that might make it interesting to the next generation but one. She has been following a Church study course on Matthew, feels that the fundamentals of what she has learned are important for her grandchildren to know, and is desperate for them to be able to participate in an informed way in her Holy Week and Easter experience.

In a way, Phoebe's experience might help her to understand Matthew's aims and intentions. He too has a clear idea of the significance of the events surrounding the first Easter and he has to find his own way of explaining that to a congregation with whose priorities and religious ideas and vocabulary he is familiar. Phoebe is learning what it means to be an evangelist.

The final section of his Gospel contains what we call the Passion Narrative. Chapters 26–8 describe the events immediately leading up to Jesus's crucifixion, and its aftermath. But we need to note from the outset that although this is the 'end' and the 'climax' of the Gospel, in a sense it is actually the beginning. Gospels, as we have noted, are sometimes described as Passion Narratives with an introduction. The Passion Narrative already existed. Assuming Mark as his source, Matthew makes very few changes to what we read in the parallel passages in Mark, at least until the crucifixion. What is different is his commentary on the events described there. We reach the Passion Narrative by a different route and so have different expectations of what we shall find there. In the preceding 25 chapters, he has set out his own interpretation and attempt at communication of these events, and although we see some stylistic similarities between these chapters and the rest, they hold few substantial surprises. They are the QED of the rest of the book.

However, in this final section, we are aware as readers that we have entered new territory. Throughout the rest of the Gospel we have got used to Jesus speaking. Sometimes he does so in long discourses without interruption. Even when there is description of an action of Jesus, more often than not it concludes with a pithy saying of his, designed to help disciples (and future Church leaders) *understand* what they have witnessed. In this long section, he hardly speaks at all. After his opening words at 26.2 (only in Matthew) he speaks briefly on only 12 further occasions until his final words in 28.18ff (also only in Matthew), to offer passing commentary on events. The disciples, who have played such a large part as the audience to his words, also fade into the background. At 26.56 they flee away, and do not reappear until 28.16. Likewise, the Pharisees are no longer the main adversaries. In this section, it is the chief priests and the elders of the nation who take their place. The addition of the word 'all' at 26.1 seems to suggest that now the teaching has finished, the commentary is over. Now is the central action. Commentators largely re-tell the story as the narrative does with little original comment, save for pointing out the meanings of symbols and allusions. They are content to let the text speak for itself.

To do

- The section we are dealing with now is chapters 26–8. Chapter 26 takes the action up till Jesus's trial by the Sanhedrin, and Peter's three-fold denial of Jesus. Chapter 27 concludes just after the crucifixion. If you feel that you are already familiar with this story, in pairs (if you are doing this as a group – or to yourself if not) tell the story as you remember it, without looking at the book. Decide between yourselves if you are satisfied that the whole story has been told, then read chapters 26–8 and see if you are right. Pay particular attention to any part of the story you may have forgotten, or anything that you had not noticed in the story before. This kind of close reading will be helpful in seeing the nuances of Matthew's account.

- Phoebe is aware that her teenage grandchildren are more used to drama and visual presentation than they are to narrative prose. She tries to find a TV or film presentation of these chapters and is surprised that *Jesus Christ Superstar* claims to be an account based on the Gospel of Matthew. She watches it again. If possible, try to do the same and, having read the text closely as above, see how well you think the screenplay achieves its stated aim. How do you interpret any changes you find?

As we have said, Matthew follows Mark's account very closely, and that could be taken as his main source. Alternatively, he may be relying on whatever was Mark's source. Though this is unlikely, it is eminently possible that a largely common form of the Passion Narrative did circulate, perhaps orally. However, Matthew could be said to have another source, and that is the Old Testament. When he is describing something for which he has no evidence, it is natural to him to conclude that what happened would have been consistent with Old Testament prediction, as he understands it, and so he sees no problem in assuming that. For example, when Jesus was praying privately in the Garden of Gethsemane, there is no way that anyone could know what he was saying – and especially if they were asleep at the time (26.36ff). And so Jesus's prayers are a kind of combination of the Lord's Prayer and Old Testament allusions.

In fact, the whole passage may well remind us of the early chapters of the Gospel, in which a tightly packed narrative is supported by Old Testament words and allusions, acting as evidence and explanation. Since we have effectively lost the voice of the principal character, we have now to pay more attention to the voice of the narrator. Literary critics remind us that only by taking the role of the narrator seriously shall we be aware of the rhetorical structure of the account, recognizing such elements as irony and paradox, which play a key part in making the story effective.

Drama and narrative skill apart, it is likely that a key question in early Christian communities, one that Gospels were written to meet (and one that Phoebe's family will no doubt immediately raise), was the question: if Jesus is the Messiah, why did he have to suffer and die? We see this incomprehension in Peter (16.22) as a representative of a wider constituency, and we might assume from the rest of the Gospel that the answer would be one that implicated the wicked intentions born of the insecurities of Jewish religious leaders. Remarks such as that at 17.12, 23.34–6 seems to place Jesus in a line of prophets who have been martyred. However, 16.20 is also a key indicator of a slightly different answer. This is the first verse of a new section of the Gospel, introduced with the words 'from that time' (cf. 4.17). It is also the first time that Jesus speaks clearly about his death, though there have been allusions such as those at 9.15 and 12.40. Peter's confession (16.16) provides the context for that. The key word (sometimes missed in English translations, e.g. REB) is the Greek word *dei*. This word means 'it is necessary', and refers to something inevitable and God-willed. The same word occurs at 26.54 at the arrest of Jesus, when again there is protest and an attempt to change the course of events. Jesus's response is that this is necessary; it must happen, and he appeals to the scriptures in support, even though, on a Jewish reading of the scriptures, there is no suggestion that the Messiah must suffer – hence the problem. While, therefore, the Jewish religious leaders may be agents of what is determined, they are not ultimately responsible.

It therefore becomes clear that the invective against Jewish religious leaders is directed at the way they interpret their role, and not as a result of their plots against Jesus. In fact, ironically, it could be said that

the belief that these people have, that they are con-
trolling events, is completely subverted by God in a
way that makes them look quite pathetic. Christian
leaders are warned not to be like them, but that is
not really the important part of the answer to the
question about why Jesus had to die. It was God's
will that he had to die, and extremely important
that Jesus demonstrated obedience in responding to
that. However, in Matthew's Passion Narrative we
do see that Matthew has continued to criticize the
Jewish leaders and widened the scope to include the
chief priests and the *elders of the nation* (my italics;
26.3). It is the Sanhedrin that makes the fateful deci-
sion, spurred on by the high priest (26.65), and it is
the chief priests and the elders who encourage the
crowd to call for the release of Barabbas (27.20).

In a passage peculiar to Matthew which embar-
rasses scholars generally, and about which they
express regret, considering its later historic implications, the people (*laos*, rather than *ethnos*, and
indeed *pas o laos* – all the people) make a declaration that Jesus's blood should be upon them and
upon their children. 'It is as shocking as it is true
that anti-Semitism accordingly became a Christian
virtue, indeed a Christian duty. After all, had not
the Jews all but wished revenge upon themselves
in the words they spoke to Pilate?' (Hagner 1993,
p. 828). While scholars also believe that Matthew's
situation in a beleaguered and possibly persecuted
Church may have influenced his expression, Minear
(1984, pp. 135–6) points out that the declaration is

made by all the people who were in the crowds, and not just Jews. He believes the passage is used rhetorically to highlight the innocence of Jesus, which is another key part of the answer to the main question. The answer must also include Jesus's words at 20.28 that he came to serve and give his life as a ransom for many, a Semitism meaning 'for all'. It is those 'many' who cheered his way into Jerusalem, greeting him as a king, who are now calling for his death. It is surely intended that Christians should identify themselves with members of those crowds. 'It is "I" who am guilty of crucifying Jesus' (Hagner, p. 828). Post-Holocaust sensibilities have rightly made anti-Semitism a key concern in modern Western society, but that may divert attention from what both Matthew and Luke do in different ways as they add to Mark's account: namely, to highlight the wider significance of this death. Matthew highlights its cosmic significance as he employs apocalyptic language and symbolism at, for example, 27.50ff. Luke makes a point of highlighting political significance (cf. Luke 23.6–12). Matthew may here be making the point that this death has repercussions in his local church context, not least in Jewish/Christian relations, an issue very relevant for his congregation.

To do

How would you understand the answer to the question: why did Jesus have to suffer and die?

Does your explanation differ from Matthew's? How important is it, do you think, for Christian discipleship that Christians have a sense of being partly responsible for Jesus's death, and how would you describe that responsibility and its implications for discipleship in, say, a Confirmation class?

To emphasize the point that the events described in the Passion Narrative had to happen, it is interesting to note the particular way that Matthew deals with Judas, after the betrayal (27.3–10). Mark makes no mention of this, and Luke's account in Acts 1.15–20 is included to highlight the necessity of having twelve apostles, witnesses to the resurrection. That account does make reference to a prophecy being fulfilled through Judas, but it is Matthew who gives the fuller account, including the last of his proof texts from the Old Testament. This is typically Matthean in that he claims the quotation is from Jeremiah, when in fact it is from Zechariah (11.7, 13). The important point here though is that Judas repents. The usual word for repentance is not used here. The word that is used has a slightly lesser force of 'regret', but interestingly it is also used in the parable of the two sons (21.29, 32). However, he cannot escape the inevitability of what he set in motion. In other words, he cannot really be blamed because he was only cooperating, though he did not know it, with 'what was necessary'. Though Matthew shows no regard for Judas (he is the only person in the Gospel who refers to Jesus as 'Rabbi'), this does have the effect of describing him effectively as collateral damage.

Although this reference to Zechariah is the last direct quotation from the Old Testament, and although, unlike in Luke's and John's accounts, Jesus says very little when on the cross, the Matthean crucifixion account is redolent with Old Testament allusion and indirect quotation. This is not usually introduced by Matthew: he has simply imported it from his source, but it is consistent with his overall approach, and reminds us of how early Christian apologetic worked. For example, the darkness covering the earth (27.45) is reminiscent of several Old Testament themes. According to Amos 8.9, darkness is associated with mourning, and it is one of the apocalyptic signs of the Day of the Lord (Joel 2.2, Zephaniah 1.15). At Exodus 10.22, darkness descended over the land (Matthew's phrase) prior to the last plague, for a period of three days, as opposed to the three hours mentioned here. The whole account (27.35–50) contains a number of echoes of Psalms 22 and 69.

To do

Read Psalms 22 and 69 and see how many references you can find that connect with the crucifixion account.

So, an answer to the question: why did Jesus have to suffer and die has three parts. The big picture is that it was an inevitable part of God's plan. Within that picture, we see that Jesus's obedience was also necessary for the plan to succeed. The Jews and Judas were also responsible in that they were the agents, though badly motivated, that put the whole sequence of events into effect. However, it is inescapable that Matthew's alterations to Mark have the effect of heightening the sense of responsibility that should be borne by the Jews. This is possibly due to the context of Matthew's Church. Verse 27.25 is the most notorious example, though, as France points out, there is no verb in the Greek, and to add it in the English translations gives a sense of enduring curse which is perhaps not contained in the original (France 1985, p. 397). There may also be a useful distinction to be made between 'the Jews' which is Matthew's designation of Jesus's opponents, and 'Israel' which is their self-designation (27.42).

If the Gospel was written in part to respond to questions about why Jesus died, it was surely also written to attempt to describe exactly **who Jesus is**. Throughout the Gospel we have seen several descriptive names and titles used. They include: Christ, Son of David, Son of Abraham, Messiah, Jesus, Emmanuel, my (beloved) Son (by God), *Kyrios* (translated as Lord or Sir or Master), Son of Man, he who is to come (11.3), the Son of the Living God, Teacher (*Didaskale*, 19.16), and 'the prophet Jesus' (21.11). This last description forms part of the account of Jesus's entry into Jerusalem. That reads like a description of a royal passage. Jesus is not explicitly named as King, though 'Son of David' might suggest that (21.9), particularly in combination with 'Hosanna', meaning literally 'save now!' The reader is invited to relate these titles to the Passion Narrative itself.

Here, the theme of kingship is much more evident, and used in ironic ways. The accusation against Jesus in the Roman court is that he claimed to be King of the Jews (27.11). Though the charge is not proven, the sentence stands, and there follows a bizarre scene in which Jesus is clothed with mock royal robes and given mock royal insignia. He is given mock obeisance, 'Hail, King of the Jews' (27.29). The heavy irony here is that Jesus is being mocked for who he really is. We are hence provided with two presentations of reality. There is the ontological reality recognizable to faith, and the dreadful physical and immediate reality of brutality and sadism. The irony continues in the succeeding passage (27.39–44) where an array of titles is bestowed upon Jesus by those who have no insight into the cosmic significance of the events they witness. They include: temple-builder, Son of God, King of Israel. The sign they erect reads 'This is Jesus', a Matthean addition, which echoes God's words, 'This is my beloved Son.' After the crucifixion, the first response comes from the Gentile Roman centurion and those who were with him (another Matthean addition to balance perhaps the mocking group of Jews).

The words 'Truly this was the Son of God' are in a sense the vindication of 24.14. They echo exactly the words of the disciples at 14.33, and although the definite article is absent from the Greek, there is clearly a technical sense to the expression.

However, those names only have relevance if we understand the expectations invested in them. This inevitably reminds us of the question, 'What did Jesus come for?' And there are firm answers contained in the rest of the Gospel. Jesus came to save his people from their sins (1.21), to proclaim the Kingdom (4.17), to teach, heal and preach (4.23, 9.35), to serve (20.28), to give his life as a ransom (20.28), and to judge (25.31ff.). By his ministry thus described he could be said to embody the Kingdom, and as Messiah he could be expected to inaugurate it. Matthew's description of the Passion certainly heightens the sense of cosmic significance of the events in a way that corresponds with what was expected at the end of the age. The entry to Jerusalem affects Jerusalem to the extent that it is 'shaken'. The verb used is *seio*, related to the noun *seismos*, both of which appear to be important eschatological signifiers for Matthew (cf. 8.24, 24.7). As the story proceeds there is a *seismos* at the crucial moment of Jesus's death (27.51, 54). 'Salvation (resurrection) is thus brought into the closest causal connection with the death of Jesus' (Hagner 1993, vol. 2, p. 850). The word is also used to introduce the single resurrection appearance (28.2 with verb at 28.4). Its significance elsewhere in apocalyptic tradition can be seen at, for example, Revelation 6.12, following the cry for vindication from the saints, and Revelation 11.13 where the bodies of the two witnesses killed in Jerusalem ascend to heaven. The Old Testament background can be seen at Isaiah 24.19, 29.6, Jeremiah 10.10 and Amos 8.8, and elsewhere. It is perhaps notable that Jesus uses the same expression at 26.45 (the hour has come) that elsewhere in the Gospel is related to the coming of the Kingdom (3.2, 4.17, 10.7, cf. 26.18 where *kairos* is used as at 8.29, 13.30, 16.3, 21.34).

To do

- Imagine yourself as a Jewish convert to Christianity, reading and using Matthew's Gospel to make sense of things. You are well versed in what the Old Testament promises. What do you think you would understand by the description contained in Matthew 27.50–4? Would you see it as a sign of the beginning of a new age, or would you see it primarily as Jesus saying something new and positive about life after death – his and yours? What do you think are the implications of your answer for Christian belief today?

- Now imagine yourself as one of Phoebe's grandchildren who have no knowledge at all of the Old Testament traditions. To make sense of this should you:

- Follow up and learn about those traditions and try to relate them to modern situations as above?
- Simply accept that the inauguration of a new age with a new vision and a new attempt to come to terms with the problem of evil in the world is basically what this is about, and, without going into detail, reflect on modern implications of that?
- Regard this as a tragic story of injustice, alongside, and comparable with, many others?
- See this as a reasonably impenetrable account amounting to a ratification of the ministry of Jesus, and pointing us back there?
- Some other response?

Other signs that Matthew groups together at the death of Jesus include darkness (cf. 24.29), and the opening of the tombs (cf. Revelation 3.10–12, 7.14–17). The response of the centurion and those who were with him is rather contrived, since they could not possibly have seen 'all that was happening'. Their response surely reflects Matthew's belief that the Gospel could convert the whole world. It is in the latter part of the Gospel that preaching the Gospel throughout the world becomes important. We have seen the reference in 24.14. There is a further reference in the commission to the disciples in

28.19, and one further interesting reference at the very beginning of the Passion Narrative.

Matthew follows Mark in placing the story of the woman who anoints Jesus at the beginning of the Passion Narrative. This seems strange to readers of Matthew, who, in comparison with Mark, makes very little reference to women. The claim made for this woman by Jesus is quite extraordinary: 'wherever this gospel is proclaimed throughout the world, what she has done will be told in memory of her' (26.13). Both Mark and Matthew include the saying of Jesus, in slightly different forms, that the women (unnamed) has done a good thing and has prepared Jesus's body for burial. Women continue to play some part in Matthew's account. Verse 27.55 refers to three women who stay to the end at the crucifixion, and then go to the grave to witness the burial. They are also witnesses to the empty grave, and the message of the angel. They are the ones who are told: come and see, and then, go and tell. All this happens when the disciples are in desertion mode, and it could be that the women feature in the story to emphasize that. Likewise, it may be that the initial story is meant to be compared with what follows immediately: the deal that Judas does to betray Jesus. One poor nameless woman shows care and love. One of the twelve is described as a heartless profiteer.

Another context, common to all the Gospel writers, is the Passover. In other words, Jesus was crucified at the religious and cultural celebration that recalled Israel's foundation narrative of freedom from slavery, and their journey to a promised land as part of a Covenant agreement with God that would determine the legal and moral basis of their society. It happened after a final plague, itself preceded by three days of darkness, in which first-born sons died. All four Gospels regard this as an important context, but there is a difference in the lessons they draw from it, and that largely depends on how it is dated. John's Gospel dates the Last Supper on the evening of Nisan 14, so Jesus died in the afternoon at the end of Nisan 14 (Jewish days are counted from sunset to sunset), the time when the paschal lambs were being killed. The feast (of Unleavened Bread, 26.17) ran from Nisan 15 to 21. Matthew therefore dates the Last Supper on Nisan 15, thus making the time that Jesus died coterminous with the freeing of the slaves (see Senior 1998, p. 290, and for a fuller discussion of the implications see France 1985, pp. 369–70).

There are other overt Passover references in the Last Supper part of the narrative, the most striking of which is the reference to the (new) Covenant signed with Jesus's blood in a clear reference to Exodus 24.8, where the ceremony to ratify the (old) Covenant involves sprinkling blood over the people. This new Covenant also stirs memories of Jeremiah 31.31–4. But quite apart from these direct references to the Passover, literary critics would urge us to find other links within the whole narrative that forms this Gospel. They might include, for example, the feeding miracles, which in turn were overlaid by the early Christian community with eucharistic significance. We might also link the Supper with the other meals that Jesus is described as having, all of which contained some teaching significance about either forgiveness, inclusiveness or the lack of privilege to those who thought they had earned it. A further reference could be the messianic banquet, which Matthew clearly has in mind at for example 22.14 and elsewhere. This opens the way for interpretations of the Eucharist as the meal of the Kingdom.

To do

If you belong to a Christian tradition that makes the Eucharist a central part of worship, how do you interpret its significance? Do any of the suggestions above widen the possibilities for you?

Among other possible Old Testament references, Matthew's interest in the Songs of the Suffering Servant is served by a number of descriptions of what happens to Jesus. There are four such songs that have been identified by scholars in the second part of the book of the prophet Isaiah. They are 42.1–9; 49.1–13; 50.4–11; and 52.13—53.12. Isaiah chapter 53 has several echoes, some of them very direct (see, for example, 53.5,7; cf. 50.6). These are not specific to Matthew, but are consistent with his themes. Another interesting example of vulnerability is provided by Jesus in the Garden of Gethsemane immediately prior to his arrest (26.36–46). This remarkable account of Jesus is one that Matthew has kept from his Markan source. It is interesting to see how Luke has used this source (Luke 22.39–42). In that account, Jesus is supported by an angel and the disciples' behaviour is explained by their grief. For Matthew the burden is emphasized by the triple repetition, is borne alone, and the disciples' behaviour is described in terms tantamount to desertion.

Immediately following the crucifixion, there is a substantial piece of narrative that belongs to Matthew alone. Part of it concerns the apocalyptic signs and the role of the women already noted. But 27.62–6 (cf. 28.11–15) describes something that may have some historical base. As we read it, however, it stands with 27.39–44 as an ironic example of how completely Jesus's opponents had misunderstood what he was talking about. Resurrection means so much more than simply emerging alive from a sealed tomb. You can no more 'disprove' the Resurrection by a false rumour about what happened to the body, than you can 'prove' it by reference to the empty tomb. Paul, who has more to say about resurrection than any other New Testament writer, makes no references to tombs.

As predicted at 26.32, the angel reiterates to the women at the tomb that Jesus will meet the disciples in Galilee. This also follows Mark, though he has no follow-up appearance. Galilee, known as 'Galilee of the Gentiles', is the most foreign part of Israel, farthest from Jerusalem. It may be, though, that is not the intended reference, but rather, a return to where most of Jesus's ministry was conducted.

Chapter 28 is peculiar to Matthew and describes that follow-up. Luke and John each have different post-crucifixion appearances. For Luke, they are all in and around Jerusalem. For John they happen in both Jerusalem and Galilee. Matthew's single appearance is given added symbolic significance by being preceded by an earthquake, and taking place on a mountain. The chapter contains two of the seven sayings in the Gospel that begin, 'do not be afraid' (28.5, 10; the others are 1.20, 8.26, 10.31, 14.27, 17.7). This is an important continuity with Old Testament 'Gospel'; see Holdsworth 2010, p. 175). Isaiah is Matthew's main Old Testament source and that book makes the good news of not being afraid a central theme, with its strongest statement perhaps in Isaiah 43.1–7. In Luke's Gospel, the first words uttered after Jesus's birth are to the shepherds: 'Do not be afraid' (2.10). Here, again, at the beginning and the end in Matthew's Gospel is the same message. A further piece of 'resolution' is the possible reference to Emmanuel (28.20).

Matthew's account of Jesus's final commission to the disciples is arguably the most majestic of the commissions in all the Gospels. It maintains the emphasis on teaching. Jesus now claims the authority which rightly belongs to the Son of Man at the end of the age. This has been a controversial claim throughout the Gospel (7.29, 8.27, 9.2–8, 10.1, 21.23–7), but is now beyond question as the new age begins. In a manner reminiscent of James Joyce's novel *Finnegan's Wake*, however, the end is but the essential prologue to the beginning. Having read the commission, as disciples, we are forced immediately, once again, to chapter 1.

To do

- Where do you think Phoebe should begin to outline the significance of Jesus: who he was and why he matters? Should it be the events of Easter? Could it be the events surrounding his birth? Should it begin with his ministry and teaching? Why do you think Matthew arranged his response as he did?
- Try to imagine all the characters from modern life who have featured in past chapters, along with Phoebe, getting together to discuss what they have learned about the Gospel. They have to prepare a short bullet-pointed response to what they have learned. What do you think that would look like?

Reading List

This list includes those books referred to in the text, together with books that will be of interest to those who want to read more about the context of Matthew's Gospel and its place in current scholarship. It is not a 'ceremonial' list of the kind sometimes found in academic books or attached to university courses, whose aim is to attempt to enhance the academic quality of the text by reference to the number of works that supposedly informed it. Each of these books has been carefully chosen to help the kind of people the book describes to find out more about Matthew.

Bacon, B. W., 1930, *Studies in Matthew*, New York, Henry Holt.

Bailey, Kenneth E., 2008, *Jesus Through Middle Eastern Eyes*, London, SPCK.

Beasley-Murray, G. R., 1954, *Jesus and the Future*, London, Macmillan.

Bornkamm, G., Barth, G., and Held, H. J., 1963, *Tradition and Interpretation in Matthew*, London, SCM Press.

Boxall, Ian, 2007, *The Books of the New Testament*, London, SCM Press.

Brown, M. J., 2000, *What They Don't Tell You: A Survivor's Guide to Biblical Studies*, Louisville Kentucky, Westminster John Knox Press.

Brown, Raymond E., 1994, *An Introduction to New Testament Christology*, London, Geoffrey Chapman.

Burkett, D., 1999, *The Son of Man Debate*, Cambridge, Cambridge University Press.

Case-Winters, Anna, 2015, *Matthew* (Belief Theological Commentaries), Louisville Kentucky, Westminster John Knox Press.

Dodd, C. H., *The Parables of the Kingdom* (revised edition 1961), London, Fontana Books.

Fenton, J., 1963, *Saint Matthew* (Penguin New Testament Commentaries), Harmondsworth, Middlesex, Penguin Books.

France, R. T., 1985, *Matthew* (Tyndale New Testament Commentaries), Nottingham, Inter-Varsity Press.

Gill, Robin, 2006, *A Textbook of Christian Ethics*, London, T&T Clark.

Glasson, T. F., 1947, *The Second Advent*, Leicester, Epworth Press.

Gowan, Donald E., 2000 (2nd edition), *Eschatology in the Old Testament*, Edinburgh, T&T Clark.

Hagner, D. A., 1993, *Matthew* (2 volumes), Word Biblical Commentaries, Dallas, Texas, World Books.

Hagner, D. A., 1999, 'The Gospel of Matthew', in M. E. Powell (ed.), *The New Testament Today*, Louisville, Kentucky, Westminster John Knox Press.

Hare, Douglas R. A., 1993, *Matthew* (Interpretation Commentaries), Louisville, Kentucky, Westminster John Knox Press.

Hill, D., 1972, *The Gospel of Matthew* (The New Century Bible Commentary), London, Marshall, Morgan and Scott.

Holdsworth, J. I., 2010, *Lies, Sex and Politicians: Communicating the Old Testament in Contemporary Culture*, London, SCM Press.

Jeremias, J., 1972, *The Parables of Jesus*, New York, Charles Scribner's Sons.

Kingsbury, J. D., 1975, *Matthew: Structure, Christology, Kingdom*, Philadelphia, Pennsylvania, Fortress Press.

Minear, Paul S., 1984, *Matthew, The Teacher's Gospel*, London, Darton Longman and Todd.

Richards, H. J., 1973, *The First Christmas: What Really Happened?* London, Collins.

Robinson, J. A. T., 1957, *Jesus and his Coming*, London, SCM Press.

Robinson, T. H., 1923/1967, *Prophecy and the Prophets in Ancient Israel*, London, Duckworth.

Saldarini, Anthony J., 1988, *Pharisees, Scribes and Sadducees in Palestinian Society*, Grand Rapids, Michigan, Eerdmans.

Senior, D., 1998, *What are they saying about Matthew?* New York, Paulist Press.

Stanton, G. N., 1992, 'The Sermon on the Mount', in J. B. Green, S. McKnight and I. H. Marshall (eds), *Dictionary of Jesus and the Gospels*, Leicester, Inter-Varsity Press.

Stanton, G. N., 1998, *Matthew* (Abingdon New Testament Commentaries), Nashville, Tennessee, Abingdon Press.

Theissen, G., 1992, *The Gospels in Context: Social and Political History in the Synoptic Tradition*, T&T Clark, Edinburgh.

Wenham, D., and Walton, S., 2001, *Exploring the New Testament*, volume 1: *Introducing the Gospels and Acts*, London, SPCK.

Wilkins, M. J., 1992, 'Discipleship', in J. B. Green, Scot McKnight, I. H. Marshall (eds), 1992, *Dictionary of Jesus and the Gospels*, Leicester, Inter-Varsity Press.

Wright, N. T., 2004, *Matthew for Everyone* (parts 1 and 2), Louisville, Kentucky, Westminster John Knox Press.

Bible References Index